D1460640

THE ULSTER DEBATE

THE
ULSTER DEBATE

Report of a Study Group
of the Institute for the Study of Conflict

CHAIRMAN
Brian Crozier
RAPPORTEUR
Robert Moss

PAPERS BY
Professor J. C. Beckett
Sir Frederick Catherwood
Lord Chalfont
Garret FitzGerald
Professor F. S. L. Lyons

THE BODLEY HEAD
LONDON   SYDNEY
TORONTO

The Ulster Debate is published by The Bodley Head in association with the Institute for the Study of Conflict.

Printed and bound in Great Britain for
The Bodley Head Ltd
9 Bow Street, London WC2E 7AL
by William Clowes & Sons Ltd, Beccles
Set in Monotype Baskerville
First published 1972

CONTENTS

Foreword
A TIME FOR STUDY

Brian Crozier

The Institute for the Study of Conflict published privately in November 1971 *The Spreading Irish Conflict* (Conflict Studies No. 17), in which Iain Hamilton narrated and interpreted a fast-moving situation and Robert Moss analysed the security problem in Ulster. There has been a continuing demand for this dual study. The Council and Director of the ISC felt, however, that there was a need for a further study of this crucially important subject, aimed at a wider readership than can be reached by the *Conflict Studies* series, which is not on sale to the general public and is available only to subscribers or on special request. The need became more urgent with the announcement, in March 1972, of the British government's new 'initiative', involving direct rule from Westminster over the troubled province.

To this end, the Institute commissioned four of the five studies that appear in this book, and convened a Study Group with the object of considering each of the papers and producing constructive suggestions. In the fifth paper, Robert Moss, as rapporteur of the Study Group, summarises the discussion, presents the findings and contributes his own views.

The guiding principle of the Study Group was realism. The outcome is a guide to the Irish problem and proposals that respect the facts and possibilities of a dangerous and delicate situation. Each paper is a separate contribution. It does not necessarily reflect the views of the other members of the Study Group.

Professor J. C. Beckett deals with the historical origins of the Northern Irish problem; Professor F. S. L. Lyons dissects the alternatives open to the governments concerned; Lord Chalfont analyses the security aspects of the situation, excluding, as far as possible, the political aspects, and Dr Garret FitzGerald considers Ireland in the European context. In a supplementary paper, Sir Frederick Catherwood presents some proposals for a long-term solution of the Irish problem as a whole. Appendices and diagrams complete the background.

Members of the Study Group

Robert Moss of *The Spreading Irish Conflict* (Conflict Studies No. 17).

Maurice Hayes
President of Town Clerks' Association, Northern Ireland. Formerly Chairman of the Community Relations Commission, Northern Ireland.

R. H. Lilley
Deputy Editor, *Belfast Telegraph*.

Geoffrey Martin
Former President of the National Union of Students; executive member of Seascope Ltd.

Brigadier W. F. K. Thompson
Military Correspondent, *Daily Telegraph*.

Northern Ireland*

J. C. Beckett

Northern Ireland, as a distinct political entity, came into being in 1920. It was a time when frontiers were being re-drawn in many parts of Europe, and long-submerged national groups were seeking and gaining a new independence. At first sight, therefore, one might be tempted to regard the creation of Northern Ireland simply as part of a general European move- ment, a typical response on the part of an imperial government to a local demand for political self-expression. But the actual circumstances were very different. The six north-eastern coun- ties of Ireland were grouped together and given a parliament and government of their own not because anyone in the area wanted (let alone demanded) such an arrangement, but be- cause the British government thought that this was the only possible way of reconciling the rival aspirations of the two Irish parties—the Nationalist (and mainly Roman Catholic) majority, who demanded self-government for the whole coun- try, and the Unionist (and mainly Protestant) minority, who wished Ireland to remain as it was, within the United King- dom. Northern Ireland came into being not because a majority of the people in the area were nationalists, but because their op- position to nationalism had, as far as possible, to be neutralised.

The forces that produced this paradoxical state of affairs can be traced far back in Irish history, and form a complicated pattern; but the essential points can be stated fairly simply. Since Tudor times, religion has been a major dividing line in Irish politics; and the Protestants, though only a minority of the population, long enjoyed a virtual monopoly of power. They were descended mainly (though by no means exclusively) from English and Scottish settlers of the seventeenth century, while the Roman Catholic majority represented, for the most part, a mixture of the old Gaelic stock with English settlers of the medieval period, a mixture, however, in which Gaelic

* A version of this paper first appeared in Volume VI, No. 1, of *The Journal of Contemporary History*.

cultural influence was very strongly marked. So long as Ireland had its own parliament, dominated by the Protestant ruling class, Protestant opinion was, naturally enough, disposed to support Ireland's claim to be regarded as a distinct and self-governing kingdom, joined to Great Britain only by the link of a common sovereign. But in the late eighteenth century, Ireland, like other parts of Europe, experienced the unsettling influence of the French Revolution; and in 1800 the Protestants, alarmed for their safety in the face of growing unrest among the Roman Catholic majority, accepted a parliamentary union with Great Britain. Their conviction that the maintenance of this union was essential to their safety was confirmed when, in 1829, Roman Catholics were admitted to full political rights. After this, any re-establishment of a separate Irish parliament would produce a radically new situation, for such a parliament would be predominantly Roman Catholic, and the Irish Protestants, instead of forming part of a permanent Protestant majority in the United Kingdom, would form a permanent minority in Ireland. It is hardly surprising, then, that the Irish Protestants as a body (though there were many notable exceptions) vigorously resisted every proposal to set up a separate parliament for Ireland, from the Repeal Campaign of Daniel O'Connell to the Home Rule movement of the Gladstonian era and the more radical nationalism of the early twentieth century.

In their opposition to nationalism the Irish Protestants had the consistent support of the Conservative party, and this support made them a powerful force in British politics. But in Ireland itself, though they enjoyed a social and economic influence out of all proportion to their numbers, the only area in which their policy commanded widespread popular support was in the province of Ulster. It was here, and here alone, that they could secure the return to Westminster of a solid body of MPs pledged to the maintenance of the parliamentary union. It was for this reason that Ulster played such an important part in the Home Rule crisis that preceded the first world war and in the revolutionary era that followed it. Protestants in the rest of Ireland were strongly organised, and their close association with the Conservative leadership made them a force to be reckoned with; but when it came to votes and, even more significantly, when it came, as it did in 1912–14, to the possibility of fighting, it was the Protestants of the north who really counted. In the last resort, the Protestants of Ulster could and would maintain their position in arms; those in the other provinces could pass resolutions and bring pressure on their friends in England; but they could do nothing on their own, either at the polls or in the field.

It was out of this situation that the idea of partition grew. As a formal proposal it certainly did not originate with the Ulster Protestants. In the 1880s and 1890s they made common cause with their fellow-Unionists in the south and west, and were prepared (in the words of their leader, Colonel Saunderson) 'to stand or fall, for weal or woe, with every loyal man who lives in Ireland'. It is true that in the critical years before the first world war they organised themselves on a provincial basis and were prepared to set up an Ulster government of their own; but by this time the idea of excluding Ulster, in whole or in part, from the operation of any system of home rule had already been suggested at Westminster; and the purpose in view was not to satisfy a spontaneous Ulster demand for independence, but to enable the rest of Ireland to enjoy self-government in peace. What the Ulster Protestants put forward was not a positive demand to manage their own affairs, but a negative demand not to have those affairs managed by a parliament in Dublin.

The proposal for partition was given statutory form in 1920 by the Government of Ireland Act. This Act created two Irish states: 'Northern Ireland', consisting of the six north-eastern counties, and 'Southern Ireland', consisting of the rest of the country. Each state was to have a parliament with limited authority over purely internal affairs, and each was to continue to send representatives to Westminster. So far as 'Southern Ireland' was concerned, the Act never became effective; and it was soon superseded by the Treaty of 1921. But in the north the Act was put into operation: elections were held, a government was formed, and Northern Ireland took its place as a distinct political entity within the UK; and this place was specifically protected by the terms of the Treaty concluded a few months later.

Though this settlement guaranteed the Protestants of the north against domination by a Dublin parliament, it was not the kind of settlement they had wanted. They had resisted home rule for Ireland; but they had never demanded home rule for themselves. What they had demanded was that they should remain as they were, that, whatever happened to the rest of Ireland, Ulster should continue as an undifferentiated part of the UK. They did not, indeed, actively oppose the Government of Ireland Act; but they regarded their passive and reluctant acceptance of it as a generous concession made in the interests of peace—to use their own term, this was 'Ulster's supreme sacrifice'. There can have been few occasions on which a politically conscious group has shown itself so unwilling to accept even partial responsibility for managing its own affairs.

In the light of the situation half a century later this may seem a strange attitude. But it must be remembered that what moved Ulster Protestants (and, indeed, Irish Protestants generally) was not nationalism, in the political sense of the word, but anti-nationalism. They had accepted wholeheartedly the fusion of Ireland with Great Britain; and, though they did not cease to be Irishmen, they believed that the best service they could render their country was to maintain unimpaired the inheritance of a common British citizenship. It is easy to see the self-interest behind this attitude; but there was a genuine conviction also. When Carson, a life-long opponent of Irish nationalism, declared to Arthur Balfour, 'It is only for Ireland that I am in politics', he meant what he said; and his career bears out the honesty of his purpose, if not the soundness of his judgment.

Northern Ireland, then, was not created to satisfy any local demand for self-government. No one in Ireland, of any political persuasion, wanted or welcomed it. Its creation was an expedient imposed on the country by a hard-pressed British cabinet, which sought only to hold two groups of Irishmen from each other's throats and to give them an opportunity of living peaceably apart, since they could not live peaceably together.

The expedient had at least some measure of success: between the early 1920s and the late 1960s Ireland enjoyed a longer period of freedom from major internal disturbance than it had known since the first half of the eighteenth century. Though the period began and ended in violence, and though the basic questions of Irish politics have not essentially altered, the interval has been long enough to bring about important political, economic, and social changes. These changes are worth examining, not just because they are bound to have a continuing influence on the future development of Ireland, but also because they illustrate, though in very special circumstances, the way in which a political structure imposed from outside, rather than developing naturally from an internal situation, can affect the life and outlook of a population.

Before attempting any examination of these changes it is necessary to indicate briefly some of the characteristics of the Northern Ireland state. Geographically, it is an artificial structure; for the six counties of which it is composed do not form a natural region. The boundary that separates it from the rest of Ireland simply follows the boundaries of the counties concerned, with the result that a division originally designed for local administrative purposes now marks an international frontier. This artificiality reflects the circumstances out of which partition emerged. When it was first seriously proposed that the Ulster Protestants should be excluded from the authority of a Dublin parliament, and when it became necessary to define the area to be so excluded, it was natural and convenient for politicians to think in terms of counties rather than to set about devising an entirely new boundary; and, indeed, such a boundary would have been almost impossible to establish on any logical basis, for predominantly Protestant and predominantly Roman Catholic areas were so intermingled that no rational line of separation could have been drawn. A later attempt to adjust the boundary as laid down in the act of 1920 came to nothing; and in 1925 the governments of the UK, the Irish Free State, and Northern Ireland concluded a tripartite agreement by which they accepted the existing division unchanged. The decision, taken in 1920 and confirmed in 1925, to draw the line of partition strictly on a county basis meant, in effect, that Northern Ireland included the largest possible area within which the Protestants could expect to maintain a safe and permanent majority. Though there were two counties, Fermanagh and Tyrone, where they were slightly outnumbered by the Roman Catholics, in the six-county area as a whole they constituted approximately two-thirds of the population.

Constitutionally, as well as geographically, Northern Ireland bears the marks of its origin. It was intended to form only one part of a compromise settlement for the whole of Ireland; and, if the compromise had worked, then Northern Ireland and 'Southern Ireland' would each have stood in the same relationship to the central government in London. The failure of the compromise has meant that the constitutional position occupied by Northern Ireland is unique, without precedent or parallel in the UK. For this reason, it is important to understand clearly just what that position is.

In the first place, Northern Ireland remains an integral part of the UK and the supreme authority of the parliament at Westminster is as full and complete there as it is in Great Britain. Secondly, the sphere within which the Northern Ireland parliament is entitled, by the Government of Ireland Act, to exercise a subordinate and delegated authority, is a very narrow one. It has no control over the armed forces, the upper levels of the judiciary, or the postal services; its authority in fiscal matters is very closely restricted, and almost the entire revenue of the province is derived from taxes imposed and collected under the authority of the UK government. Thirdly, Northern Ireland's freedom of action is, in practice, still further limited by the financial position. The Government of Ireland Act provided that UK revenue collected in, or attributable to, Northern Ireland should constitute a separate fund, to be put at the disposal of the Northern Ireland parliament; and it was supposed that this, together with the small amount of revenue that that parliament was authorised to raise on its own, would not only suffice for all the needs of the government but would also leave a surplus to meet Northern Ireland's share of common UK expenditure. Even if this was an accurate assessment of the position in 1920, economic depression on the one hand, and the rising cost of government on the other, made it quite unrealistic later on. Northern Ireland, treated as a distinct financial unit, could not possibly afford the same standard of social services as obtains in the rest of the UK. To meet this situation the terms of the act of 1920 have, in practice, been modified; and Northern Ireland receives, out of the general revenue of the UK, funds sufficient to maintain its social services at the same level as the corresponding services in Great Britain. This system of subsidy can be justified on two grounds. In the first place, since the people of Northern Ireland are UK citizens, taxed at the same rate and under the same authority as their fellow citizens in Great Britain, they have a right to the same social services. In the second place, the parliament of Northern Ireland is so restricted in its powers that it cannot take the steps that an independent government might take (e.g. by controlling foreign trade) to shape its own economy. While fiscal policy is effectively controlled from Westminster it might seem not unreasonable that Northern Ireland should share the same benefits as well as the same burdens as other areas in the economic unit of which it forms a part. But, though these considerations have, in practice, been accepted by the UK government, it is not necessarily bound by them; and no Northern Ireland cabinet can afford to overlook the fact that a less sympathetic attitude at Westminster could have crippling financial consequences for the province.

In origin, then, Northern Ireland represented an area artificially carved out, and containing a divided population, with a substantial minority utterly opposed to the whole transaction; while even the majority, on whose account the transaction had been conceived, were obliged to accept a new constitutional system that they had not asked for and did not want. And this was a system, moreover, that imposed on the local government responsibility for administration while withholding the powers essential for the development of an independent economic and social policy. What kind of Northern Ireland has emerged from such a beginning?

A cynic might be inclined to assert that nothing that has emerged is new, and that Irish politics stand precisely where they stood half a century ago. In a very general way, there is some truth in this assertion. The two great questions that have dominated Ireland since the seventeenth century are still with

us: the internal question of the relations between Roman
Catholic and Protestant; the external question of the relations
between Ireland and Great Britain. But though these questions
may remain the same in essence, they have altered very considerably in form; and the main cause of the change is to be
found in the operation of the political system imposed on the
north of Ireland by the Coalition government in 1920–22.
For this reason, the internal development of Northern Ireland
has a more than local importance; but, for this reason also, it
cannot properly be understood except in relation to the larger
issues of Irish and Anglo-Irish politics.

Two factors, both implicit in its origins, have dominated the
life of Northern Ireland. One is, that it was established to
satisfy the claims of the Ulster Protestants. Not, indeed, in the
way they wanted, and not so much for their own sake as in
order that the government might be free to come to terms
with the rest of the country; but still, it was a settlement intended to placate Protestant fears. The other is, that neither
the Roman Catholic minority in the north, nor Irish opinion
generally, ever wholeheartedly accepted the settlement as just
or final. Despite the tripartite agreement of 1925, successive
Dublin governments continued to demand that the border
should be abolished and all Ireland brought under their
control; and these demands received the support and kept
alive the hopes of the northern nationalists.

In these circumstances, it was not unnatural that the
Protestants should feel themselves in constant danger of
attack, and should be inclined to regard every Roman Catholic
as an actual or potential enemy. Their fears were not wholly
unreasonable. In the early 1920s the IRA (Irish Republican
Army) had mounted a formidable offensive against the new
regime, and had made its strongholds in the predominantly
Roman Catholic areas; and the ten or twelve Roman Catholic
members elected to the Northern Ireland parliament consistently advocated that the six-county area should be brought
under the Dublin government. To the average Protestant it
seemed that the only safe course was for Protestants to stand
firmly together in order that they might keep a tight grip on all
the organs of political power and, as far as possible, on all the

means of economic and social influence. Thus the two religious groups had no sense of common loyalty or common purpose to counteract their age-old tendency to live as separate communities. On the contrary, the establishment of Northern Ireland had the effect of sharpening their differences and increasing their mutual fears and suspicions.

And yet, despite all this, the mere continued existence of Northern Ireland as a separate political area with its own administration, gradually produced changes of outlook. The Roman Catholics were obliged to recognise that the new regime, if not permanent, was at least unlikely to be quickly overthrown; and, though they did not abandon the hope of Irish unity, their first concern was now to press their special claims, particularly in the field of education, upon the Northern Ireland government. Nationalist MPs did not cease to be nationalist in principle; but their most direct concern was to represent and defend the interests of the minority. Thus, though they did not accept the role of a formal opposition, or offer the prospect of an alternative government, they were drawn into the political life of Northern Ireland, and their immediate, if not their ultimate, aims were determined by local circumstances.

Among the Protestant majority a change of outlook came more easily and was much more unambiguous. In 1920 they had regarded the new regime designed by the British government with suspicion, not unmixed with resentment; and during the next few years a cry of 'Back to Westminster' was occasionally raised. But it was not long before they discovered that there were substantial advantages in having a parliament of their own, in which they were assured of a permanent majority; and their new control of the administrative machinery, and especially of the police, gave them a degree of influence that they had not possessed in the past, when British governments and British officials had been reluctant to accept the view that the 'loyalty' of Protestants gave them a claim to special consideration. Besides all this, the existence of a separate constitutional system in the north of Ireland, though they had disliked it at first, offered them protection against the danger that could follow from a change in the party politics of Great

Britain. It would be difficult now for any government there, however sympathetic it might be to the claims of Dublin, to modify the existing settlement against the wish of the Northern Ireland parliament.

Very quickly, then, the Protestants forgot the reluctance with which they had accepted the Government of Ireland Act. They were pleased with the power and the measure of security that their new position gave them; they were inclined, now, to congratulate themselves on their semi-independence; and they soon developed a sort of 'Ulster patriotism'. This was something more than a local pride in their region and its special characteristics, such as had existed in the north long before 1920, just as it had existed, and still exists, in all parts of the British Isles. But here there was a conscious association of land and people with a sense of political power and political achievement. The very use of the term 'Ulster' as equivalent to 'Northern Ireland', which was common among Protestants, though it was often no more than a sacrifice of accuracy to convenience, could carry significant overtones. It gave the new state a kind of continuity with the past; it implied that it represented a recognised and well-established territorial division; and it associated Northern Ireland with those stirring seventeenth-century events that were always alive in the folk-memory of Ulster Protestants. Here we have already a kind of embryonic nationalism; or, at the least, a state of mind out of which a sense of national, rather than merely regional, distinctiveness might, in certain circumstances, emerge.

There was nothing at all in this 'Ulster patriotism' to appeal to the Roman Catholics. But they too had to adjust themselves, though for different reasons and with very different feelings, to the new situation. And both groups, though they continued to form separate communities, divided by long memories and mutual suspicion, had at least this in common, that their immediate political horizon was now bounded by the six counties of Northern Ireland. Within this area they were obliged to exist side by side; and some sort of understanding had to be reached, some kind of *modus vivendi*, however precarious, had to be worked out. Inevitably, the Roman Catholics suffered. They were not only a minority, but a poor minority. Though the legal framework of the old 'Protestant Ascendancy' had been dismantled a century earlier, the balance of wealth remained heavily on the Protestant side; and the continuing sense of difference and hostility retarded any natural process of levelling out. Even if the average Roman Catholic had not found the idea of an 'Ulster patriotism' repulsive on other grounds, he would have seen little in his material position or prospects to inspire pride in the government under which he lived.

If one looks at Northern Ireland in isolation one would be inclined to condemn both majority and minority as short-sighted. Should not the Unionist government, instead of relying exclusively on Protestant support, have made every effort to win the adherence of Roman Catholics? Should not the Nationalist opposition, instead of acting, in fact if not in name, as a Catholic party, have broadened its basis and put forward a comprehensive programme calculated to appeal to Protestants, so that in time it might have been able to supply a viable alternative government? These strictures are not without weight; and if Northern Ireland were indeed isolated they would be almost unanswerable. But, as things are, one cannot fairly assess the position except in the general context of Irish and Anglo-Irish politics; one must look at Dublin and at London, as well as at Belfast. The Dublin government's opposition to partition and, in particular, the claim (embodied in the 1937 constitution) that the six-county area was, *de jure*, part of the Irish state, had a double effect in the north. Most obviously, it kept alive Protestant fears that the settlement of 1920 might yet be overthrown; and the constant anti-Unionist propaganda emanating from Dublin did more than anything else to maintain Protestant solidarity and to keep the Unionist government in power. But the Roman Catholics too were affected by the policy of Dublin, for it kept alive among them the hope that the territorial unity of Ireland would, sooner or later, be re-established. They could not be expected to disown this hope; yet any expression of it only served to confirm the traditional Protestant belief that Roman Catholics were not 'loyal'. So long as the 'Border question' remained alive it was

bound to have a dominant influence in politics; and Dublin
was not prepared to let it die.

The internal situation in Northern Ireland has necessarily
been influenced by the fact that it is part of the UK. The
defence of the border (which is almost as much an internal
as an external question) is, of course, a matter for London,
not for Belfast; and an Act passed at Westminster in 1949,
after the declaration of an Irish Republic claiming jurisdiction over the whole island, specifically guarantees the
maintenance of the existing constitutional position unless and
until the majority in Northern Ireland desire a change. But
the influence of the UK connection appears in other ways
also. In particular, it has meant that the standard of social
services is very much higher in the north than in the rest of the
country. The difference is, indeed, so great that the inclusion
of Northern Ireland, now, in an all-Ireland state would present
enormous social and financial problems. At the time of the
Home Rule crisis of 1912–14 the industrial north-east was one
of the more prosperous areas of the British Isles; today, like
some similar industrial areas in Britain, it has become a liability, and a liability that the rest of Ireland could not afford,
unless the standard of living were to be drastically reduced.

This state of affairs is uncomfortable for both Unionists and
Nationalists. The Unionists are reluctant to admit that
Northern Ireland cannot pay its way, and they are uneasy at
the restrictions imposed by their financial dependence on Great
Britain. The Nationalists have to face the fact that if they
achieved their aim of union with the Republic they would be
materially worse off than they are. But these considerations,
however unwelcome, cannot be ignored; and they have influenced attitudes on both sides during the present crisis.

The crisis itself arose, paradoxically, out of a real, though
very gradual, approach towards stability. By the middle 1960s
Northern Ireland had been in existence for more than forty
years. Only the elderly could have any clear recollection of a
different system. The Dublin government, for all its propaganda, seemed more and more inclined to accept the existing
position, and public opinion in the Republic had almost
ceased to trouble itself about the border. The utter failure of the

IRA campaign in the 1950s suggested that the days of vi͏̯
were past. Among Ulster Protestants there was a growing
who felt that the union could be maintained without reli͏̯
on the old sectarian war-cries. Among Roman Catholics there
was a new readiness to accept Northern Ireland as, for all
practical purposes, a permanent fact. In some areas, at least,
their economic position was slowly improving; and everywhere
they felt the benefit of the welfare state. It seemed not impossible to believe that at last Northern Ireland was approaching a condition in which all its citizens could feel a common
interest in promoting a common prosperity.

Two factors, not unusual in such a situation, brought about
the reversal of this hopeful trend—impatience on one side and
fear on the other. Among the Roman Catholics, and especially
among the young, there was a strong feeling that they had
waited too long, and that the government must be forced to
meet their complaints, especially about discrimination in
housing and employment. Following the examples set in
America and France, they sought to gain their end by public
demonstrations; and their action provoked counter-demon-
strations by Protestants. It would, indeed, have taken time
and patience and skilful leadership to educate the Protestant
masses in a new attitude of mind. They had been so long taught
to believe that the safety of the state depended upon their
solidarity and supremacy, so deeply imbued with the idea that
every Roman Catholic was an enemy, that they could hardly
be blamed for regarding any gesture of conciliation as 'treason'.
Thus, once again, the two sections of the population were
ranged against each other in what, but for the intervention of
the army, would have been open war; and the Ulster position
seemed to have turned back to 1920.

And yet this appearance is deceptive. The agitation for
'Civil Rights', with which the crisis began, was not a demand
for union with the Republic, though Protestant alarmists were
ready to interpret it in this sense. Indeed, the leaders of the
agitation might be regarded as more unionist than the
Unionists, for they claimed that all they sought was 'British
standards' of administration. How far the Civil Rights agitation was fomented, encouraged, or used by other groups—

Republican, Communist, Trotskyite, Maoist, Anarchist—is a matter of dispute. But, to begin with at least, the point at issue was not the continued existence of Northern Ireland, but the way in which it was to be governed; and those who led the campaign for reform found their most effective allies in London, not in Dublin.

A fifty-years' existence has not given Northern Ireland either unity or stability; but it has defined the political, economic, and social problems of the area in specifically local terms. Even if 'Northern Ireland', as a separate political entity, were to be abolished, it would, in a real sense, survive, and carry into the foreseeable future the characteristics that have developed from the settlement imposed in 1920.

The Alternatives open to Governments

F. S. L. Lyons

When this paper was first circulated for discussion at the end of February it consisted of a survey of the alternatives open to the three governments which were at that time involved in the Irish crisis. I began by making the point that although their policies could not be viewed in isolation, it might make for clarity if they were considered separately. Now, of course, the three have been reduced to two, but I still feel that a tripartite division of the subject will be helpful, at least to the extent that it will enable us to look at this complex situation as it should be looked at—from the three vantage points of London, Belfast and Dublin. In order to avoid repetition I have discussed what might be described as general issues in the section dealing with the options available to the British government; inevitably, therefore, that section is much longer than the other two.

1. The British Government

To predict what further or ultimate steps the British government may take to end the crisis in addition to the direct rule imposed at the end of March is almost as hazardous as it was to predict at the end of February that direct rule would be imposed at all. In fact, in the first version of this paper, after weighing as carefully as was then possible the pros and cons of direct rule, I came to the hesitant conclusion that it would be such a dangerous nettle to grasp that the government might well yield to the temptation to try some other, less forthright, manœuvre. In the end—and, on the whole, to their credit—they decided to make their leap in the dark and we have therefore now to reckon with a situation which has been profoundly changed, even if the actual extent and direction of the change remain, at the time of writing, an enigma. I say 'profoundly changed' because, while it is true that Stormont has only been suspended for a year, hardly anyone believes that it will re-emerge in its pristine shape. It may re-emerge in a greatly changed form, it may vanish from the earth, but that it can ever again become the Stormont of old seems beyond the bounds of political possibility. Nevertheless, although direct rule has clearly altered the framework within which an ultimate, even an interim, solution must be sought, it is well to remember that in and of itself it provides no solution, whether interim or ultimate. It is still possible for the British government to take either a negative or a positive attitude, to swing towards disengagement or towards further and more constructive involvement, but whichever way the choice may fall, the necessity of decision is no less imperative than it has been for the last two years. Each of these two paths out of the present impasse needs to be explored.

(a) Disengagement

Although direct rule of Northern Ireland from London through the agency of a Minister of State may seem at first glance to be at the opposite pole from disengagement, it can be argued that in reality it is, or in certain circumstances could be, a staging-post towards disengagement. I say this because I find it difficult to conceive of direct rule as other than a very temporary expedient destined to last only until some more permanent and far-reaching settlement can be worked out. From a British point of view direct rule without a reasonable prospect of general agreement in a foreseeable future would merely constitute a perilous addition to an already intolerable burden. For what direct rule really implies is the destruction of the buffer-state which has hitherto borne the brunt of the battle. The destruction of that buffer-state has, for obvious reasons, been a major objective of the IRA campaign, but only as a first step towards the reunification of Ireland. Any prolonged British delay in acceding to their full demand could quite conceivably have the effect of directing their energies towards this island. That would not necessarily be a reason for recoiling from direct rule and the government, in imposing it, have presumably counted the cost and found the risk acceptable. All the same, an outbreak of bombing in Britain—if not now, at whatever date in the future might seem to the IRA most likely to pay dividends—remains both a theoretical and a practical possibility. If it were to happen, it is only reasonable to suppose that it would intensify the already keen desire of many ordinary men and women that the Irish should be left to their own incomprehensible devices.

The movement of opinion towards disengagement does not, however, depend solely upon the conditions to be created by a bombing campaign which has not happened yet, and may never do so in the future. On the contrary, it is the beginning of wisdom to realise that such a movement of opinion has already begun and that, whatever public policy may be, the view is very frequently expressed in private that the proper course for Britain is to 'withdraw'. Unfortunately, and as with nearly everything in Northern Ireland, different people mean different things when they use the same word. For those who oppose the British presence there, 'withdrawal' means primarily the withdrawal of the army, though this, it seems, can be either partial or total. By 'partial' is often meant withdrawal of the troops from the Catholic areas—particularly in Derry and Belfast—as a means of reducing tension and thus clearing the way for an attempt at a political solution *before* the troops were removed from the rest of the province. Total withdrawal means what it says—that *all* troops should withdraw from the *whole* province—but usually with the qualification that the operation should be 'phased' and not precipitate.

It is doubtful, at this point in time, whether the distinction between partial and total withdrawal any longer has much meaning. True, there is a kind of partial withdrawal already, in the sense that troops normally stay out of 'no-go' areas such as 'Free Derry', but those whom this is designed to placate will not be satisfied with such half-measures. Yet to proceed to whole measures is fraught with grave dangers. Indeed, withdrawal without a previous settlement would be a policy of despair; it does not need much imagination to see what the likely consequences of premature disengagement could be. Protestant restraint, hitherto maintained behind the screen of the army, might soon reach breaking-point and IRA and Unionist would be left face to face. Since the immediate victims of such a confrontation would be the Catholic minority, it might very well happen that the south would be drawn in and that Ireland would at last be involved in a much more fundamental civil war than the one between the pro- and anti-Treaty forces fifty years ago.

It would not, however, be a clear-cut civil war, because the stereotyped rivalries between north and south, Catholic and Protestant, Nationalist and Unionist, would be complicated by a probable split within the IRA as to the ultimate objective of the struggle.* The country as a whole might conceivably face a period, perhaps a long period, in which it would become a battleground for contending factions, allying with and opposing each other in an endless kaleidoscope out of which eventually might emerge a 'strong' government, of the right or of the left, ruling by virtue of its ability to impose and enforce peace, and counting parliamentary democracy among its first victims.

From an Irish viewpoint this is an unutterably bleak prospect and it is not surprising that Dr Cruise O'Brien in the *Observer* of 6 February should have written despairingly of 'alternative routes to the cemetery'. But at the moment we are concerned with the British viewpoint and it is necessary to insist that the worse the Irish situation becomes the more seductive the notion of total withdrawal is likely to be. Moreover, in such circumstances it would be naive to suppose that withdrawal would merely connote military withdrawal. If the departure of the army were to precipitate the kind of collapse in Ireland I have just been describing, the effect of this would surely be to reinforce the quite natural, but hitherto repressed, desire of sensible, but deeply confused Englishmen to cut their losses and let the Irish stew in their own juice. Indeed, it is a source of constant astonishment to me that this kind of reaction has hitherto been so little in evidence. When one reflects upon the amount of British money spent in Northern Ireland since the war, and upon the British lives lost there in the last two years, it is very difficult to explain the dogged endurance by public

* This split already exists and to some extent reflects the preoccupation of the 'Official' IRA with the ideal of achieving a Workers' Republic, and the attachment of the 'Provisional' IRA to a more traditional form of militant nationalism. The exigencies of war have tended to drive them closer together during the past year, but sharp differences remain and these could at any time again result in open warfare between them.

opinion of a state of affairs which, in more volatile countries, would long ago have been rejected as intolerable.

I'm afraid I find it difficult to accept as a sufficient explanation of this forbearance that Northern Ireland is defended because it is constitutionally a part of the United Kingdom or that people's hearts instinctively warm to Belfast as being indistinguishable from Birmingham. This may be a natural assumption for Ulster Unionists to make, but any Irishman living in England must long since have become aware that the attitude towards the present crisis of most of those whom he meets is compounded in roughly equal parts of disgust and bewilderment. To the extent that men and women encountered casually in conversation support the army's role in Northern Ireland at all, they often seem to do so out of an inarticulate but deeply-held feeling that, precisely because it *is* a war, the army ought to be supported and that if it were to be withdrawn this would be an open admission of defeat, and therefore wounding to a national pride which is not quite so vestigial as is often supposed.

Such a mood might sustain the government for a while—though it is unlikely to persist without an occasional victory to nourish it—but one must presume the government's own resolution not to pull out would stem from more sophisticated calculations. I was never inclined to number the various pledges given over the years to the Northern Ireland government as among the more crucial of those calculations. Indeed, not merely as an historian, but as an Irishman one-half of whose family was Southern Unionist, the more fervent the British protestations against disengagement the more I would tend to question them. The fact that the government to which the protestations have been made in the past now no longer exists is not exactly reassuring, at least for those to whom the maintenance of the British connection is almost literally a matter of life and death.

Nevertheless, there are substantial reasons why withdrawal should not be complete or precipitate. Politically, such action would be a very serious blow to prestige, since it would indicate to the world at large that Britain was no longer able to keep order in what is, constitutionally speaking, a part of the

UK. And while the economic saving to be made from a complete severance of the Ulster connection would no doubt be tempting, it is perhaps not altogether cynical to suggest that a Conservative government with a very small majority might find a handful of Ulster Unionist votes in the House of Commons too painful to part with.* Such an argument would obviously cut the other way with a Labour government; on the other hand, if the Irish voters in Britain are to continue their traditional attachment to the Labour party, that party is unlikely to strain their allegiance by leaving their compatriots and co-religionists to the fortunes of civil war in Ireland unless driven to it by extreme necessity.

There are, of course, other factors which operate against withdrawal. If the British departure from the scene were to produce the chaos in Ireland which has so often been predicted, a vacuum would thereby have been created into which other interested parties might seek to enter. This has been the fate of other weak and divided small countries and there is no reason to suppose that St Patrick has secured for Holy Ireland a special dispensation from the norms of power-politics. An Ireland reduced to the status and condition of a Cuba or a Haiti would not be an agreeable neighbour for Britain. Still less would this be so when the implications of simultaneous entry into the Common Market would seem to involve closer rather than looser relations between the two islands. No doubt this aspect of the question will be dealt with by Dr FitzGerald, so I will content myself here by observing that while it would presumably be possible for the Community as a whole to cut Ireland adrift without too much difficulty or compunction, I find it hard to believe that Britain's role in the Community, or indeed her own economy, would not be adversely affected by an Irish slide into anarchy.

---

* If it be objected that the government is much too high-minded to think of such mundane considerations at this critical time, then I shall be only too glad to stand corrected. But it is worth pointing out that if four Ulster Unionists had voted in the Common Market division of 17 February as they voted last October, the government majority would have been in danger. Three of the four switched votes and one abstained; all had previously voted against going into Europe.

(b) Closer Involvement

If, for these or other reasons, direct rule does not point towards disengagement, but rather towards closer involvement in the affairs of Northern Ireland, what conceivable forms might that involvement take? All answers to this question must remain speculative for the time being, since nothing has yet emerged from Mr Whitelaw's administration to suggest the lines of a future settlement. All that can be said with certainty so far is that his evident intention has been to isolate the IRA by a progressive reduction of internment and by keeping the army as much as possible away from provocative situations. It is presumably Mr Whitelaw's hope that by this policy he may regain the confidence of moderate Catholics to such an extent as to enable them to come to a conference table when the time is ripe.

A great deal will obviously depend upon how rapidly and how completely Mr Whitelaw can achieve this goal. But no less will depend upon whether he can do it without a massive alienation of the Ulster Unionist majority. And here we are in the presence of a mystery as yet unexplained. When direct rule was instituted and Mr Faulkner's government disappeared almost overnight it was widely predicted—indeed, I expected it myself—that there would be a formidable Protestant 'backlash'. Yet in the event all that happened in the immediate aftermath of direct rule was the Stormont demonstration and the two-day strike. It would, of course, be entirely premature to deduce from this that the much-vaunted backlash will never be more than merely verbal froth and fury. Until the British government's long-term plans for the province are unveiled who can say to what lengths Ulster Unionists might not in certain circumstances be goaded? I shall return in the next section to this question of their possible reactions, but it will be relevant to consider here—from the British viewpoint—one suggestion which has recently received considerable Unionist support, that the logical corollary to direct rule is a complete integration of Northern Ireland into the UK. One can see that this would have a certain atavistic appeal for some Ulster Unionists, since it would bring them full circle to the position occupied by their forefathers in 1913 and 1914, when exclusion from a Dublin-based Home Rule parliament was taken to mean continued inclusion of a variable number of Ulster counties in the UK along the lines laid down by the Act of Union over a hundred years earlier.

It is exceedingly doubtful, however, whether complete integration of this kind would have many attractions for British politicians of any party. It would make the alternative of disengagement more difficult to adopt should it ever become necessary in the future. It would bring the Northern Ireland question still further into British life when the dearest hope of many people is that, if they wait long enough, it will eventually go away. Worst of all, perhaps, it would bring it into British life not just in the sense of putative IRA bombs, but of actual Irish members of parliament attending in increased numbers at Westminster; and although they would no doubt be divided between Unionists and Nationalists, the prospect of an endless series of Irish debates in the nineteenth-century tradition, and still more the possibility of crucial issues depending on a handful of Irish votes, are sufficiently depressing to cause both Socialists and Conservatives to think long and hard before hanging such an albatross around their own necks.

On the other hand, if direct rule is only a temporary expedient, and if disengagement and integration are both unacceptable, what alternatives can be offered in their stead? Between a majority pledged to the British connection and a minority pledged to its severance there seems no common ground. Yet, if civil war is not to happen sooner or later some sort of accommodation must be found. If it is to be found—and the outcome still hangs in the balance—then the key may possibly lie in attempting to impose a sequence upon events rather than, as hitherto, struggling to catch up with them. This means in effect that Westminster must pursue a short-term and a long-term policy simultaneously. On the short term, it must still continue its efforts to restore peace in the province, but it must also move further and faster towards bringing interned suspects to trial and it must persevere with the initiative already taken by Mr Whitelaw in releasing those against whom no charges can be brought that would stand up in a court of law.

The main objective of such a line of approach must obviously be to bring responsible Nationalist and Catholic leaders to the conference table, and especially the leaders of the Social Democratic and Labour party. If Mr Whitelaw can convince them that he means business then he might possibly, just possibly, be able to persuade them to talk *without pre-conditions*, but equally *without limitations*, as to what might, or might not, be put on the agenda.

It is at this point that a long-term policy should emerge alongside the short-term policy. For if no items are barred from the agenda it is quite certain that on the nationalist side the reunification of Ireland will be a primary consideration. It is hard to see how the British government could encourage anyone to believe that such a goal was possible in the near or middle future without goading the Protestant majority in the north to such fury that civil war would be unavoidable. On the other hand, it is legitimate to doubt that the majority of nationalists north or south seriously believe that reunification could happen overnight. But they do need to be convinced that it would not once again be shelved after the immediate violence had subsided. Ideally, therefore, one would wish to see the British government propose to all the interested parties that they should begin to think about a political structure in Ireland very different from the present structure and designed to come into effect at an agreed date in the future. So that that date would not be indefinitely postponed a British declaration of intent to withdraw the army in carefully phased stages might simultaneously be made.

What possible future structure can one envisage for Ireland? My paper is not intended to engage in constitution-mongering for any part of the country but in concluding this section it may not come amiss to suggest that among the matters to be considered the following might be expected to find a place:

(i) The question of timing. If there is any validity in the idea that both an interim and a permanent settlement have to be worked out, it is only common-sense to realise that the 'interim' may have to last for a period of years while a long-term solution is sought at what may well be a whole series of conferences.

(ii) If conferences are to be held, the question will arise as to who should attend them. Technically, no doubt, only governments can sign treaties and only parliaments ratify them, but the present Irish situation will not be resolved if such peace proposals as may emerge are not submitted in one way or another to all interested parties. Conceivably, this, or part of it, could be done by referendum, but I cannot see how direct consultation can be avoided, nor indeed how, if the army does not quickly win a decisive victory, extremists, whether of the right or of the left, can be excluded from such consultation. It will be objected, with reason, that governments cannot negotiate with the representatives of those who have sought, or may seek, by violence to overthrow the constitution. But to the historian this argument wakens an ironic echo. Lloyd George and his coalition said much the same thing in 1920, yet the following year they sat down at the table with the 'murder gang', as they had described them, and negotiated the Treaty. The parallel, however, is not exact. The men who negotiated the Treaty in 1921 may, in British eyes, have been the representatives of an illegal institution, Dáil Eireann, but it was nevertheless an institution which had been elected by the Irish people. This cannot now be said of either of the branches of the IRA or of Sinn Féin, though of course it is conceivable that a general election in either part of Ireland in a still fluid political situation might produce a militant party, or parties, of significant size, in which case consultation with more or less extreme groups might become a necessity rather than an indulgence; the same presumably would be true if a significant right-wing Unionist party were to emerge from an election in Northern Ireland.

(iii) It will obviously be difficult to get even constitutional parties round a table to discuss a long-term and permanent solution, but, given time, there is no reason why constitutional lawyers should not devise a workable mode of procedure. In the meanwhile they could do worse than re-examine Mr Wilson's proposals of last November for a Constitutional Commission representative of governments and parties from the three areas involved; and although circumstances have obviously changed much since then, there is still a good deal in the fifteen points he then put forward which would repay careful study.

(iv) During the interim period, although security would still almost certainly have to remain a UK responsibility, a main aim of policy would be to ensure Catholic participation in those areas of government—for example, housing, employment, education and welfare—in which they feel a particular concern. Whether this were to take the form of increased weight in a reconstructed Stormont, elected by Proportional Representation and with revised constituency boundaries, or of some more limited experiment in 'community government' or 'community administration' would be a matter for discussion and, one would hope, early and urgent discussion. But the exact mode of Catholic involvement, though obviously important, is for the present of less moment than that the proposals should be sufficiently generous for Catholics to be able to return to the political arena with some real assurance of a more hopeful future. This has become more difficult since the Derry shootings at the end of January, but that very event has made it more imperative.

(v) While the interim arrangements were in force it would be highly desirable, indeed essential, to develop as many contacts as possible between north and south. Various expedients have been suggested, but the one which recurs most persistently is the proposal, embodied in the Government of Ireland Act but never implemented, that a Council of Ireland representative of the two parliaments should be established. This need not at the outset exercise the modest powers entrusted to it by the Act. The important thing is that people from opposite sides should meet, that they should discuss matters of common concern, and that, in due course, recommendations from the Council should achieve sufficient authority as to afford a basis for common legislation by the two Irish parliaments; this assumes, of course, the continued operation of some form of Northern Ireland parliament.

(vi) If the concept of an interim settlement is accepted, then of course it follows that the prospects and scope of a permanent solution must always be held in mind. It would be vital for the Republic to use the interim as a period during which steps would be taken to make membership of a common polity more attractive to Ulster Unionists. These would presumably include a revision of the Constitution so as to remove matters offensive to northern Protestants, and also a strenuous effort to achieve parity in the social services. Whether the pious hope is justified that common membership of the European Economic Community would work in the same direction I have left it to Dr FitzGerald to determine.

(vii) Even if direct rule were to give place to some form of community government as part of an interim solution, the long term intractable problem would remain. It would still be necessary to find some constitutional framework within which the Protestant majority could live in harmony with their neighbours while retaining their own self respect. Innumerable suggestions have come from many quarters as to how this infinitely desirable objective might be achieved. Two of these seem to recur with more than ordinary frequency. One—which has been developed in some detail by Mr Richard Ryan, TD, in *Irish Times*, 12 February 1972—is that Britain and the Republic should exercise a condominium over Northern Ireland; the other is that a provincial parliament should be recreated within a federal, or confederal, system for the whole of Ireland. Both proposals bristle with difficulties, as indeed do all others. A condominium presents obvious complexities in the sharing of sovereignty and the delimitation of spheres of influence, while in *Conflict Studies* (No. 17, November 1971), Mr Moss has emphasised the obstacles in the way of establishing a federal structure. Nevertheless, although the difficulties inherent in such suggestions are certainly formidable, the situation is too grave for either of them to be rejected out of hand. At the very least, it is essential to investigate as fully and as sympathetically as possible how much regional autonomy can be exercised within such a structure. It is to be presumed, however, that until the conditions for some solution of this kind had been created, Northern Ireland would continue to be a part of the UK and would be entitled, as hitherto, to look to London for help towards economic recovery and for the maintenance of existing standards of welfare.

(viii) The assumption in the previous paragraph is that

Northern Ireland cannot be coerced into joining an all-Ireland republic. To assume otherwise would be to confront the south with the same sort of problem, though on a still larger scale, as that which the Stormont government has hitherto failed to solve. On the other hand, though Ulster Unionists are a large minority in Ireland viewed as a whole, they are still a minority and the same question can be asked of them as presumably they ask of their existing Catholic population—how far can dissident minorities frustrate the will and defy the authority of majorities bent on exercising power? Although I believe that no satisfactory union will ever occur in Ireland except upon a voluntary basis, all the governments concerned presumably will have to reckon with the possibility, or likelihood, of Ulster resistance to reunification being as intransigent at the end of the interim period as at the beginning. In a last desperate effort to avoid the civil war that might then threaten, recourse might just conceivably be had to the device that was intended in 1921 to deal with this very predicament. I am referring, of course, to the possibility of appointing a Boundary Commission. The precedent is not a happy one, as I am well aware, but after many years of deadlock is it not possible that Unionists might not actually welcome an opportunity to shed some of those districts which have been both an economic and political liability? Admittedly, this would not solve the problem of Belfast (which might in the end have to be dealt with by the even more extreme method of population transfer), but a Unionist government wedded to preserving a Protestant outpost of the UK might at least consider whether Derry City and certain other border areas are worth the price which is having to be paid for them at this moment. The tragic consequence of this would be that to revise rather than to remove the border would be in effect to recognise the permanence of the division between two kinds of Irishmen. Perhaps that division *is* permanent and unsurmountable, but since little thought has been devoted in the last half century to overcoming it, it seems to me quite wrong to assume, as a rigid law of politics, that Ulster Unionist intransigence would remain for ever unmoved if constructive policies were at last to be tried.

One has only to put such proposals on paper to realise how visionary, or how naive, they must appear to those who are caught up in the crisis. They do not exhaust the possibilities and they are not themselves all necessary elements in an ultimate solution. But, since that solution will have to be made by Irishmen in Ireland, the British government might reasonably be said to have discharged its responsibilities if it made it clear (1) that the present situation can no longer continue; (2) that while it will not coerce Ulster Unionists into a unified Ireland, it would welcome any moves in the south which would make reunification ultimately palatable to the north; (3) that the interests of northern Catholics must be safeguarded in the short term and that in the long term their aspiration to join their co-religionists in the south must be seriously considered; (4) that the period during which Britain can hold the ring is now a limited one and that by a fixed date it will be for Irishmen to reconcile their differences or fight each other to the death.*

2. Northern Ireland Attitudes

If I deal more briefly with the situation which prevails in Northern Ireland at the moment of writing, that is not because I regard this as anything other than the heart of the matter, but simply because some facets of the problem have already been mentioned previously in this paper.

The most obvious point to be made is that Northern Ireland still runs true to form in confounding all the predictions that

* Since this paper is devoted primarily to the options open to governments, I have not attempted to analyse the Irish policy of the Labour opposition. It is broadly true that, while it was possible to speak of a bipartisan approach in the earlier stages of the crisis (though even then only at the cost of some over-simplification), the attitude of the Labour Party has latterly diverged fairly sharply from that of the Conservatives, especially since internment. Both parties are of course opposed to solutions through violence, but it seems clear from various statements, and especially from Mr Wilson's very specific proposals last November, that Labour, if in power, would seek a far-reaching and long-range solution. Probably also, though this is hypothetical, pressure within the party for a more positive approach to reunification is likely to increase.

have been made about it in the past. For months before direct rule was imposed the air was filled with dire prognostications about the fearful Protestant backlash which the British government would elicit if it dared to proceed to this extremity. Yet, as we saw earlier, the backlash has so far not materialised, though this is not to say that it will not materialise in the future. The most immediate effect of direct rule upon Protestant opinion seems to have been to induce stunned bewilderment rather than outright resentment. Indeed, one may go further and suggest that in some quarters relief may have been the predominant emotion. This bewilderment, it must be said, is by no means a Protestant monopoly and one reason why direct rule may be regarded as having secured a breathing-space (though not, alas, a halt to the killing) is precisely because it has obliged all sections to rethink their positions and this, besides being for some a painful business, cannot be a quick or easy business for any.

In considering the various shifts in attitude which are apparently taking place at this moment, it is only natural that we should begin with the Unionists, since it is to them that direct rule has presented the greatest challenge. How are they to meet it? At present three, possibly four, reactions seem to predominate, but it is well to remember that this kind of fragmentation would be unlikely to persist if the violence in the streets were to continue unabated or if Ulster Protestants had reason to fear that they were being, or were about to be, compelled into a shot-gun marriage with the Republic.

One of the reactions to direct rule has already been mentioned and need only detain us briefly. This is that the proper course is to carry the British connection to its logical conclusion and press for full integration. This concept, to which the Rev. Ian Paisley has given the weight of his authority, is bound to attract support from what one might call traditional Unionists, as well perhaps as from some who had habitually regarded the activities of Stormont as being no more than peripheral to their own lives and interests. After all, it would emphasise the British connection, it would banish the spectre of Irish reunification and it would comfortingly recall the good old days before those vexatious Home Rulers began to tamper so dangerously with the Act of Union. I have already suggested reasons why such a return to the womb would not arouse great enthusiasm in Britain. Here I would wish merely to register my doubt whether integration would really serve the purposes of those who argue for it. It might indeed serve those purposes if there was any real guarantee that it was likely to be permanent. But even if it could be assumed that a Conservative government which has already jettisoned some of the safeguards most cherished by Ulster Unionists would bind itself for an indefinite future to maintain the full integration of Northern Ireland with the rest of the UK, there can certainly be no expectation that a future Labour government would agree to do likewise, especially since some sections of the party are decidedly sympathetic towards Irish reunification.

If, then, integration were to be refused (or if it were to be conceded and then after a few years found to be undesirable or unworkable) we might expect a reaction of another kind from that section of Ulster Unionists whose memories go back to the 1912–14 crisis (which, indeed, they are in no danger of being allowed to forget) and who might, if pressed hard enough, resort to independent action. But to do so would be to ignore a fundamental fact about Northern Ireland's existence. This is that its existence depends not so much upon British bayonets (which, conceivably, in a dark hour, might be replaced by those of the Vanguard movement, or some equivalent body), but upon the elaborate structure of economic subsidy and benefit which has given the province such prosperity as it has been able to attain in recent years. Withdraw this financial support and the result can scarcely be other than chaos. It is this factor more than any other which militates against the last, desperate throw of the dice which Mr Craig and/or his associates might be goaded into attempting—some form of UDI. Upon this notion the recently reported response of a former Northern Ireland minister is the best comment: 'Where's the money? Where's the ideological justification?' Precisely so. A regime which opted for independence as a means of demonstrating its loyalty to the Crown might be paying homage to the shades of its ancestors, but it would find it difficult to defend its logic before the bar of world opinion.

Much worse, a regime which, in opting for independence, drastically reduced the living-standards of its supporters, might before long find those supporters exceedingly thin on the ground.

This is not to say that a Protestant backlash, whether leading to UDI or not, is to be ruled out. On the contrary, it is a major and recurring theme of this paper that it is a real possibility if angry and anxious men are driven too far too fast. And if Mr Craig himself were to draw back from the abyss at the last moment, there might well be others to take his place. Who can tell what mute, inglorious Carson may even now be waiting in the wings?

UDI is such an extreme and final gamble that it is probably safe to say that only monumental mishandling of the situation would be likely to provoke it in the foreseeable future. But there remain two other possible stances, each to some extent shrouded in present mystery. One is the attitude of the Alliance Party. This, which aims at grass-roots co-operation with Catholics—in fact at taking sectarianism out of politics—and which has an undoubted, and possibly increasing, appeal to moderate opinion, is not mysterious as to its policy, only as to its destination. Although it seems recently to have made some small inroads on official Unionism, it will be impossible to tell what its standing in the community really is until there is a general election. And even then much would depend upon the climate in which that election might be held. If the climate were extreme, then the Alliance Party would probably fare ill. If it were mild, then the party would still have to contend with those Unionists, and they are many, who, though far from being hard-liners, are nervous of, if not hostile towards, co-operation with Catholics.

By official Unionism (though the phrase, like the concept, may now be obsolescent) I mean that section which is still probably the strongest section—the section which gave its support to Mr Faulkner when he was Prime Minister and which, in all probability, still stands loyally behind him. It would be a great mistake to suppose that because he and his cabinet have suffered the oblivion which usually overtakes fallen ministers that their role is now finished. On the contrary, they could have a crucial part to play in the future, not least if Mr Faulkner himself were to occupy a seat at Westminster, where, from a Unionist viewpoint, his conspicuous abilities are certainly badly needed.

But his attitude, and that of those who follow him, is bound to be enigmatic so long as the further intentions of the British government remain unknown. If the border question is not pushed into the foreground, and if the prime emphasis is placed on securing the re-entry of Catholics into the political and administrative life of the province, then we might reasonably expect the former ministers to play a part in this kind of reconstruction. After all, it is proper to recall that their own record of reform was much more impressive than their critics have ever been prepared to concede, and although some of their measures have of their nature been slow to take effect, it would be surprising if a further drive towards better community relations did not receive some support from them. This might not be the case if communal co-operation were conceived of in terms of ministers representative of the different communities sitting together in a cabinet responsible to a rejuvenated Northern Ireland parliament; while still in office Mr Faulkner and his colleagues made it quite clear in their Green Paper of October 1971 that they thought this was unrealistic. But a short-term programme of administrative co-operation which did not attempt to ape cabinet government, combined with a long-term federal solution which took account of the fears and wishes of the northern majority, might together prove enough to bring the official Unionists back into active politics.

All of this, however, would depend upon factors which are largely outside the control of Unionists, regardless of their individual affiliations. It would depend in the first place upon whether, and how soon, the forces of the Crown can restore peace and security in the streets, and this in turn on whether, and how soon, the government initiative can isolate the IRA from the moderate Catholic population. In the first weeks of direct rule there were signs that this might be happening. The two wings of the IRA themselves appeared to be taken off balance by the government's move and it even seemed as if they might come under considerable civilian pressure to abandon, or at least to modify, their campaign. For the moment this erosion of support seems to have been checked (sometimes, no doubt, by intimidation thinly disguised as persuasion) and the shootings and bombings continue. On the other hand, the progressive relaxation of internment, and the deliberately conciliatory stance adopted by Mr Whitelaw, have certainly begun to restore some degree of Catholic confidence in the government's longer term intentions, though in the aftermath of the Derry shootings there is a long, hard road to travel. This confidence can scarcely be expected to burgeon until internment is finally ended—that is, after all, the criterion by which most Nationalists continue to judge British sincerity. But once it is ended it would be reasonable to expect both that the situation of the IRA would become more difficult and also that the SDLP would be able to play the crucial role which must surely be theirs in the future. It must be stressed, however, that the battle against the IRA must be expected to continue and that it will not be possible to dispense with a strong, *and active*, British military presence until the province has again been made safe for its citizens.

Upon the restoration of order and upon co-operation between moderate Unionists and moderate Nationalists the hopes of Northern Ireland, indeed of all Ireland, mainly rest. But whether the future of the province will lie in maintaining some form of permanent connection with Britain, or in a slow and tentative approach to the Republic, will depend not merely upon the stamina of either Ulster 'loyalism' or of the IRA, but also upon the leavening effect of the changes already, or about to be, effected and above all, perhaps, upon the Republic showing a more constructive and imaginative attitude towards the problem of partition than it has done hitherto.

3. The Government of the Republic

I have been asked to add a note on the options open to the Republic, but, although this is obviously an important factor in the situation, I shall be as brief as possible in the knowledge that there will be other parties to the debate who are much better qualified than I to deal with it.

I suppose what strikes one most forcibly about Mr Lynch's position is how little room he has in which to manœuvre. Mr Lynch has many difficulties but I think it would be fair to say that the worst of these do not stem only, or even perhaps primarily, from the smallness and precariousness of his parliamentary majority, frequent source of anxiety to him as that must be. His worst problems seem to me to be of two kinds—one internal to his own party, the other arising from the balance of power within the country, a balance which would create a tense situation no matter what party was in office.

The internal problem—the problem peculiarly applicable to Fianna Fail—is that it started its career nearly fifty years ago as the party of frustrated revolution, but has been for the last forty of those years *par excellence* the party of government. Inheriting from its remote past an ideological commitment to the achievement of an all Ireland republic, it is vulnerable to charges of inconsistency, 'betrayal', etc. These can, indeed, be rationally answered, but at a time of acute and highly charged crisis, rational answers tend to go unheeded and there have been ample indications of the extreme difficulty Mr Lynch has had for the last two years in keeping his party together. That he has succeeded so much and for so long is a remarkable achievement which has, I think, been under-rated in Britain. But he may not go on succeeding for ever and it has from time to time appeared as if he was increasingly being carried along in the wake of events without much apparent capacity to control them.

His freedom of manœuvre is limited externally, as it were, by the fact that the Irish government does not appear to dispose of sufficient force, or sufficiently reliable force, to take serious action against the IRA. This is a situation which may change—before Derry there were signs that it was beginning to change—but the inability of his government to deal sternly with the private army (or armies) within their territory has clearly been a grave limitation upon Mr Lynch's power to develop a more positive policy. Assumptions (which I must admit to sharing myself until recently) that because the country has become more prosperous in the last ten years, or because it was being faced with the crucial challenge of entry into Europe, people would have too much to lose by becoming involved in a political unheaval, seem to me now to be fallacious in that they overlook the possibility (or likelihood) that a prosperous and peaceful community may be *more* rather than less vulnerable to pressure from an armed and determined minority.

But this is precisely where the transforming effect of the Derry shootings has made its impact. Up to that time, although the northern crisis had caused increasing anger and anxiety in the Republic (intensified after the internment policy had been adopted), it is probably not unfair to say that most people, though of course sympathetically concerned about their co-religionists in Northern Ireland, were at least as much concerned about the possibility of violence spreading south of the border. The majority were not and are not interested in the ideal of a 'workers' republic', but they know enough about modern Irish history to want to keep the gun out of their own domestic politics.

No doubt this is what most ordinary people still want, but all the evidence that came out of Ireland immediately after 30 January suggested that we were in the presence of a convulsion of popular feeling which powerfully recalled the effect of the 1916 executions. More recently, it would seem, feeling has somewhat subsided—it is by no means absurd to regard the burning of the British embassy as an act of catharsis—but the feeling has been shown to exist and it could be exacerbated again by any untoward event; Mr Lynch can hardly be unaware of this and it can only have the effect of further limiting his capacity to manœuvre. Up to the time of the shootings, whatever intransigent noises he might make towards Mr Faulkner or Mr Heath—and after internment they had become markedly more intransigent—he would, if pressed, have probably still been prepared to say that while reunification ought certainly to be on the agenda, the immediate and over-powering need was to improve and to protect the position of Catholics in the north. And in the sense that time would be needed to make the Republic a more attractive place to Ulster Unionists—in terms both of welfare benefits and of individual and religious rights—a gradualist approach towards the abolition of the border made perfectly good sense.

It may be that if the next weeks or months see a significant reduction in violence this kind of gradualism may once more become a feasible policy. At the moment, and given the state of feeling in the Republic, gradualism or, at any rate overt gradualism, would be for Mr Lynch a policy of suicide. Willy-nilly he has now to compete with the IRA. He can only do so by insisting that reunification must form part of an ultimate settlement and that in such a settlement the Republic must play its part. This does not necessarily rule out a return to gradualism—much depends on how 'ultimate' the ultimate settlement may be—but Mr Lynch will scarcely be able to move far in that direction until he has been able to demonstrate the authority of his own government in his own country. And whether he can do that will turn mainly, I suspect, on events over which he can have little control—will depend, in the last resort, upon the terms offered to northern Catholics, on their readiness to accept them, and on the willingness of Ulster Unionists to concede them. To maintain his contacts with the parliamentary opposition in the north, to seek to strengthen the rule of law at home, and to press in London for a conference to find a permanent and all-Ireland solution—these seem to be the principal if limited options open to him.

There remains one further alternative which, though it lies technically outside my brief, ought at least to be mentioned. This is the possibility that Fianna Fail may after all crumble from within and that Mr Lynch's exiguous parliamentary majority may therefore disappear. What the result of the ensuing general election might be no one can predict. It cannot, indeed, even be predicted that it would follow normal democratic lines. As crucial as any that has been held since 1932, or even 1918, it would certainly be tense and might be violent. But suppose Fianna Fail did not achieve an overall majority or suppose the election proved impossible or undesirable to hold. Would there in the first instance be a coalition based on an alliance between Fine Gael and Labour, or would there—in the event of a closely disputed election or of no election at all—be a national government in which all three main parties would join? If so, would it have any policy other than to preserve the stability of the state? Would it be possible for the members of such a government to agree upon a policy for the north? Would they, in the final analysis, be able to reach a common mind about the Irish problem in its wider ramifications? I do not know the answers to these questions and am content to leave them in the void. Perhaps the unfolding of events will make it unnecessary even to ask them. But in Dublin, as in Belfast and London, one has an oppressive sense of sands beginning to run out. And one hopes with a kind of desperation that at this point in history nobody needs to be reminded that in Ireland time's wingèd chariot is generally jet-propelled.

The Balance of Military Forces

Lord Chalfont

*But if truth makes not her way into the understanding by her own light she
will be but the weaker for any borrowed force violence can add to her.*

John Locke

Any serious analysis of the military balance in Northern
Ireland must begin with the *caveat*—indeed the *cliché*—that
the problems of Ireland will not be solved by military means
alone. This is not to say that the British Army cannot defeat
the IRA. Even within the limitations imposed upon the actions
of the government forces, it is demonstrable that the security
forces have the capacity within a reasonable time-scale to
restrict urban terrorism to a level which need not indefinitely
inhibit constructive political discussion. Certainly before the
incident at Londonderry on 30 January, and the change in the
political situation which followed, they were well on the way
to doing so. *Without* those limitations, they could undoubtedly
destroy the IRA as an effective force, but at an unacceptable
political cost, since some of the limitations are the inevitable
and acceptable corollary of internal military operations in an
open democratic society; while others spring from actions and
political pressures within a sovereign foreign power with which
the United Kingdom has relations which might be described,
technically at any rate, as friendly. In any case, as Mr Robert
Moss has written in his admirable book *Urban Guerrillas*, the
survival of a particular political system—and it is that and
nothing less which is at stake in Northern Ireland—depends
not merely on the balance of forces, but on whether it is
possible within the existing political system to satisfy legitimate
demands for reform.

To discuss such a possibility is not within the scope of this
essay, the purpose of which is to analyse the military aspects
of the situation and to consider how it might be possible to
create a situation in which constructive political arrangements
have a reasonable chance of success. It will, nevertheless, be
necessary to discuss certain political factors, to the extent that

they bear upon the military balance. It is proposed to approach the problem by considering the overall threat to the security of the area—not only from urban terrorism by the IRA, but also from the possibility of communal conflict or even civil war in Ulster; by assessing the capacity of the government forces in various circumstances to contain and defeat the threat; and by taking account of the effect on the equation of the policies of the government of the Republic of Ireland. The threats to security arise from a number of possible situations which might arise separately or in combination. The present situation, involving the IRA in urban terrorism against the government security forces; an emerging anti-IRA 'backlash' by Protestant organisations, which is beginning to involve the security forces in an attempt to separate the conflicting factions; and the final, if remote, possibility of military intervention across the border from the South.

The principal immediate threat is the Irish Republican Army—the IRA, and it might be useful to consider very briefly the history of this somewhat melodramatic organisation, not only by way of a traditional introduction, but also because each confrontation in the development of the Irish problem has its own specific lessons for the present crisis. In various forms and under different names, the IRA has been active for a hundred years or more, but it was with the Easter Uprising in Dublin in 1916 that the story really begins. This was a war of independence, and in one sense it succeeded; the IRA did not defeat the British Army but they brought about a failure of will in the British government which led to withdrawal from Ireland. Just as important as this simple fact was the manner of its achievement. It was not the military efficiency of the IRA which led to the British disengagement—although 3,000 IRA men tied up over 50,000 British troops, police and auxiliaries and killed 600 of the security forces at a cost of 750 to themselves. *It was rather that IRA propaganda succeeded in creating in London a total disenchantment with the war and in winning sympathy for the revolutionary cause elsewhere in the world.* Some of the propaganda undoubtedly contained more than a grain of truth—the Black and Tans were not as scrupulous as today's security forces—but it would be unwise for anyone trying to

find, in 1972, the truth behind the atrocity stories to forget
that violent rhetoric and cynical propaganda is as familiar
a weapon in subversion as gelignite or the sub-machine gun.

Another significant aspect of the IRA's victory was that it
was, of course, incomplete. Like EOKA in Cyprus forty years
later, they had the spoils of war snatched from them by what
they regarded then—and clearly still regard—as a shameful
political compromise. The Government of Ireland Act of 1920
and the Anglo-Irish peace agreement of 1921 provided for
the partition of Ireland; a situation endorsed in 1925 by a
tripartite agreement signed by the Governments of the United
Kingdom, the Irish Free State and Northern Ireland. This,
however, was not achieved without a civil war in which the
IRA murdered Field-Marshal Sir Henry Wilson in London,
kidnapped the assistant chief of staff of the Irish Army and
blew up the Four Courts in Dublin. The *dail* authorised trial
by court martial and after a series of military executions on
conviction of carrying arms (including that of Robert Erskine
Childers); and a number of summary executions without trial
(including that of Rory O'Connor, who had blown up the
Four Courts), a measure of order was restored. It is, in the
context of today's crisis, significant to note that more than
10,000 people had been imprisoned, about 50 had been exe-
cuted and the normal process of law had been almost entirely
suspended before the IRA could be persuaded to desist from
violence; and all this by the Government of Ireland.

Apart from the murder of Kevin O'Higgins in 1927 which
led to the proscription of all revolutionary societies as treason-
able, there was comparative stability until 1938, when De
Valera concluded a treaty with the British which involved the
withdrawal of the British naval forces which had remained in
Ireland under the 1921 treaty; the British Government,
however, refused to consider any revision of the policy of
partition and the IRA now transferred its attention from
'the traitors in Dublin' to England and Northern Ireland. A
series of explosions took place in Belfast and in English cities,
including the incident of August 1939 in Coventry, when five
people were killed. Once again the brief campaign seems to
contain, at least for those willing to learn, some lessons for

the present. It was the ludicrous incompetence of the terrorists rather than any deliberate intent which led to casualties from the primitive bombs scattered indiscriminately about the lavatories and telephone boxes of London and Belfast; and the deaths, more than the destruction, dissipated the public sympathy without which no terrorist organisation can survive. The government of the UK, preoccupied with a more serious enemy, and the government of Ireland, concerned with economic survival, took advantage of this to ensure that effective measures were taken against subversive activities. The measures were firm and decisive.

Since the war the IRA, possibly believing that Ulster would prove a softer target than either England or the Republic, has directed its attention mainly to the North. In the 1950s their gunmen crossed the border from the Republic and attacked military barracks and training establishments in Londonderry and Armagh; these raids, together with a partially abortive attack on the Officers' Training Corps of Felstead School in Essex, provided the arms for a border campaign that began in December 1956. It was a catalogue of technical blunders and tactical incompetence; many of the explosive devices either failed to work at all or they blew up in the faces of the terrorists—the first of what the security forces have now named, with macabre soldier humour, 'own goals'; and in 1962, having totally failed to enlist the support of the Catholic population in the North, the IRA gave up with an almost audible sigh of relief. Mao-tse-tung's image of the guerrilla fighter who moves among the population like a fish in water had its grim application to the gunmen from the South—they were particularly clumsy fish, but their main, and predictably fatal deficiency was a shortage of water.

The present crisis really began in the autumn of 1968 with the clashes in Londonderry between Civil Rights demonstrators and the Royal Ulster Constabulary. Since then the situation has deteriorated by way of a confrontation between Catholics and Protestants, with the British Army brought in to keep them apart, to a direct campaign of terrorism with the IRA once more emerging as the principal threat, although this time divided into two factions—the Official and Provisional

Wings. It is this situation with which we are now concerned. To the British government and to the majority of British people the problem is a simple one of armed subversion. They take the classic view that no democratically elected government can submit to violence or the threat of violence and survive; that negotiation with armed terrorists is out of the question; and that therefore violence must end before any attempt is made to redress the grievances of the insurgents. In the familiar idiom of operations in aid of the civil power, it is for the security forces to restore the rule of law and create a stable situation in which the normal political processes can be resumed. To the IRA and their supporters the problem is one of colonial oppression in which a substantial part of Ireland is occupied by a foreign power, and in which helpless minorities are deprived of civil rights and made the victims of economic, social and religious discrimination. In other words they are, in accordance with their own rather subjective view of history, completing the task which the politicians prevented them from completing in 1922.

Both these attitudes are in fact over-simplified. On the one hand, however brutal and often outrageous their methods may sometimes be, to treat the IRA solely as thugs and psychopaths is not only unconstructive, but dangerous, since it ignores the political grievances which would remain even if the security forces were able to clear the terrorists from the streets tomorrow. On the other hand the IRA's conception of themselves as single-minded colonial freedom-fighters is not entirely borne out by the facts. For some time the Official IRA and its political counterpart Sinn Fein have been for all practical purposes under Marxist leadership. It is not too extreme to argue that the reunification of Ireland is irrelevant in the context of their fundamental aim of eroding and eventually destroying the existing political and social order in both parts of Ireland—and eventually in the rest of the UK as well. They are, in effect, not a nationalist movement, but a revolutionary 'popular front'. It was principally for this reason that early last year the Provisional IRA emerged to provide a greater appeal to recruits, being an active militant force, with more limited political aims. It rejects the international communist leadership of the Official IRA in Dublin and has consistently maintained the primary political aim of the unification of Ireland and abolition of the Stormont government. At the time of writing the official IRA has discontinued terrorist activities, leaving the field to the Provisionals. The byzantine internal politics of Irish terrorist organisations do not prevent them from agreeing on one crucial matter. Both wings of the IRA have, for their own different reasons, the same immediate aim—to create a failure of will in the British government which will lead to a withdrawal from Ulster. The first question to be asked, therefore, is: are they capable of achieving this aim? To answer the question it is necessary not only to assess the relative strengths of the terrorists and the security forces, but also to take into account the tactics and morale of both sides, and finally to discuss the impact on the confrontation of extraneous factors—notably the capabilities and intentions of the Protestants and the attitudes and actions of the government of the Republic of Ireland.

To deal first with the IRA in the North, the overall strength of the Provisional Wing immediately after internment was implemented was estimated to be a little over 1,000. Of these, between 500 and 600 could be described as activists engaged in organised operations of armed terrorism. 400 of these were operating in Belfast—still one of the main centres of IRA activity in the North. This comparatively small force was organised into three cells, rather grandiloquently known as battalions—the 1st Battalion in the Upper Falls area, Turf Lodge and Anderstown; and 2nd Battalion in Ballymurphy and the Clonard; and the 3rd Battalion, at that time virtually eliminated by the security forces, in the Market area. An IRA battalion organisation includes Company Commanders, Quartermasters, Education Officers, etc., but the main operational group is the ASU, or active service unit, a 5–8 man cell normally operating to a large extent on its own and without much in the way of central leadership or control.

The Official Wing was about 750 strong and of these about 330 were active terrorists, including about 160 operating in Belfast. In addition there were small groups in the border areas, amounting to possibly 150 in all, the largest group (40) being based in Dundalk. Their general organisational pattern is similar to that of the Provisionals. Both wings have been substantially weakened by the operations of the security forces, and especially by the effects of internment and interrogation. Whatever may be the balance of the political and moral arguments about imprisonment without trial and 'interrogation in depth'—and these must certainly be taken into account in any attempt to formulate a plan for the future—the flow of information which they produced was dramatic. At various stages during the internment programme the Provisional Wing was deprived of about 600 officers and volunteers, including 470 in Belfast. The Official Wing lost about 200. As the Parker Report on interrogation has made clear, a mass of information about personalities, morale, tactics and organisation came into the hands of the security forces; and the massive haul of arms, ammunition and explosives is illustrated in the table at Appendix A, showing the amounts discovered by the security forces before and after internment was put into effect.

While the internment policy was fully in force, therefore, the active armed terrorist strength of the IRA in the North was between 900 and 1,000. Leadership became generally speaking poor and morale was eroded by the success of security force operations. Unless hard-core terrorist leaders are released from internment the situation is unlikely to change substantially. The IRA are armed with sub-machine guns, carbines, pistols and rifles, with a few light machine guns and rocket launchers. Gelignite and other high explosives are used to manufacture mines, nail bombs and grenades. Many of the explosive devices used to destroy buildings and other property are equipped with quite sophisticated time-fuses and anti-handling devices.

In the South the IRA has between 1,500 and 2,000 members, organised into small groups in each of the 26 counties. The location of most of their training areas is known and training goes on systematically. Control is divided almost equally between Provisional and Official Wings. An important function of the IRA in the South is to train Ulster terrorists for operations in the North and to provide an escape and safe refuge organisation for IRA men on the run from Ulster, of whom there are usually about 150 at any one time.

Around this dedicated, ramshackle, but quite effective terrorist hard-core are a number of sympathisers and co-operators, whose strength and commitment to the cause varies with the political and military climate. The normal situation in the South is that about 10% of the population can be counted on to be sympathetic to the IRA, while something like 3% are actively co-operative. In the North—especially since internment, the publicity surrounding interrogation methods, and the deaths in Londonderry on 30 January—the Catholic support for the IRA has been massive and it has included a number of organisations which are, in effect, support groups for the main terrorist units. The most important of these is the Catholic Ex-Servicemen's Association; a curiously named body of men since it draws its recruits from people who have not necessarily served in any known military organisation. It claims a strength of 10,000, is probably more like 2,000 strong in fact, and its main bases are in Belfast, Londonderry and Newry, where its function is to 'protect' the Catholic areas. It is, needless to say, comprehensively penetrated by the IRA.

The Youth Wing of the IRA, known as the Fianna na Eireann, is gradually being brought into the front line. Its strength is very difficult to assess as it consists very largely of children and teen-age hooligans who have in the past been used either in provocative mob action, designed to draw British troops into IRA ambushes and killing areas, or as an early warning system to alert terrorists in hiding of the approach of security forces. Recently, however, they have been used in armed terrorist operations and bombing incidents—a sinister development since security forces are naturally reluctant to shoot at children, even if they are armed; and similarly the government is normally inhibited from interning or imprisoning children for terrorist activities. Women also play an important part in IRA operations, giving warning of the approach of security forces, providing intelligence, and giving shelter to IRA men in hiding from the Army and the police.

The Northern Ireland Civil Rights Association, between

500 and 600 strong, is in everything but name an IRA organisation. It is firmly in the grip of Cathal Goulding's Official IRA, itself strongly Marxist-orientated. The Provisionals' counterpart is the Northern Civil Resistance Movement, a loosely organised and comparatively ineffective group.

It is evident from this situation that the present terrorist campaign is fundamentally different from those of the 1920s, the 1930s and the 1950s. It is now concentrated single-mindedly against Northern Ireland. (The tragically incompetent attack on the Parachute Brigade Headquarters in Aldershot was almost certainly an isolated attempt at reprisal for the Londonderry incident of 30 January.) The present terrorists are comparatively well armed and, although they still display a compulsive tendency to blow themselves up from time to time, they are generally speaking ruthless, often atrociously cruel, although in some cases physically courageous. Of the two wings of the IRA, the Provisionals have in the past been noticeably more militant than the Officials; on the other hand their leadership is defective and many of their recruits are social rejects or young tearaways in search of escape from the grinding urban squalor of Londonderry and Belfast. A recent significant development has been a change of leadership in the Official organisation in the North, leading to more violent and militant tactics by its members. Most important of all, the IRA appears to have, for the present at least, the support of the majority of the Catholic population of the North.

Facing this threat is the Royal Ulster Constabulary and a substantial British Army garrison. For all practical purposes the situation has until now been completely in the hands of the Army and its General Officer Commanding, Sir Harry Tuzo, who is in overall operational control, and whose general directive comes straight from Whitehall. The Royal Ulster Constabulary, 4,000 to 5,500 strong including reservists—it had been hoped at one time that the composition of this force would be one-third Catholic, but this has in fact not been achieved—is unable to carry out normal police duties in many Catholic areas. However, it conducts joint patrols with the Army and has a number of mobile Special Patrol Groups.

Similarly, the Ulster Defence Regiment, formed to support the regular forces in Northern Ireland, operates mainly in the rural areas and is not suitable for crowd control or riot duties in urban areas.

The British Army in Northern Ireland, on the other hand, is a highly organised, well trained and powerfully equipped force, currently numbering some 15,000 officers and men. It is organised into three brigades of varying sizes and at present consists of two armoured reconnaissance regiments and 17 units operating in the infantry role. These are mainly Infantry Battalions from the Army's regular order of battle, but they include also units of the Royal Armoured Corps, Royal Artillery, Royal Engineers, the Royal Marines, the Royal Air Force Regiment and other supporting arms and services. Their leadership is of a very high order, their morale has always been high, and with the help of the Special Branch of the Royal Ulster Constabulary they have built up a reasonably comprehensive intelligence picture of the IRA organisations.

If, therefore, the confrontation were simply one of strength and military efficiency, the security forces would have a decisive superiority. However, as the operations in Cyprus, Malaya, Vietnam and Kenya have clearly demonstrated, a relatively small number of determined irregulars can often bewilder and frustrate security forces many times their size; largely because their aim is *not* to inflict a decisive defeat on the government military forces but, as General Grivas wrote in his *Guerrilla Warfare*, 'to win a moral victory, through a process of attrition, by harassing, confusing and finally exasperating the enemy forces with the effect of achieving one main aim . . . ', the main aim, of course, being to bring about a breakdown in military morale and a failure of will in the government.

Tactics are crucial to the achievement of this aim. The basic objective underlying the tactical plan of the terrorists must be the support of the local population. Without it, no subversive movement can hope to succeed. For the IRA this virtually rules out sustained operations in most parts of the countryside which in Northern Ireland is largely Protestant. The Catholic ghettoes are in the towns of Belfast, Londonderry and Newry;

and it is here that the IRA must seek its support; it is here, for all practical purposes, that the terrorists must operate. After the first phase of inter-communal rioting was over and the IRA began to concentrate on the British Army, their initial tactics were based on street riots, often used as a cover for sniper fire. At this stage the IRA were no match for the Army, and in October 1970 a programme of systematic bombing and selective assassination began. This included the killing in March 1971 of three soldiers of the Royal Highland Fusiliers outside the Squire's Hill Tavern in Belfast. The violence grew to a climax in Belfast and Londonderry until August 1971 when the policy of internment was put into effect. The sudden removal of many of their more experienced leaders seemed to demoralise the terrorists whose reaction was an unco-ordinated recourse to indiscriminate bombing and open confrontations with the security forces. After a week of this, the IRA reverted to the more familiar tactics of selective assassination and bombing. Later the pattern of violence underwent a change. Under mounting pressure in Belfast from soldiers operating on fresh and accurate intelligence, the IRA were forced to transfer their attention to Londonderry and the border areas and the number of shooting and bombing incidents in Belfast began to decrease. The monthly total of security incidents in Northern Ireland, which had risen to over 1,000 in August 1971, was down to 765 for the month of December; the number of bombings had gone down from 242 in September to 181 in December, while the weight of explosives captured or made harmless had risen from 390 lb to 770 lb. The Army had, by the end of 1971, begun to believe that they were capable of bringing the situation under control. Since the end of 1971 the pattern has—with notable exceptions such as the Londonderry incident and the week of intensive violence which followed it, the Parachute Brigade explosion and the Abercorn Restaurant massacres in Donegal Street—continued in this now familiar pattern of shooting, ambushing and bombing, although the frequency of incidents is again being intensified.

It is possible to conclude, with some certainty, that if the confrontation had continued unchanged by extraneous factors, the IRA would have been defeated to the extent that they would have failed for the time being to achieve even their most limited political aims. On the one hand the government accepted that it would never be possible, even using the most oppressive counter-measures, to create a situation in which it would be possible to guarantee total absence of violence. The isolated explosion and the selective assassination would always be possible except in a security system unimaginable outside a police state. On the other hand the IRA knew that they had failed to make even the slightest impression on the morale of the security forces, and that unless the armed forces could be defeated or demoralised, the government was unlikely to submit to the campaign of violence. The assumption of direct rule by the Westminster Government, the suspension of Stormont and the release of a number of internees has, of course, introduced a new factor into the equation. So far it has had no substantial impact on the level of violence and it has crystallised the problem of the 'no-go' area—typified in the Creggan and Bogside areas of Londonderry where the IRA are in complete control. So far the attitude of the government has been that to mount a clearing-out operation on these areas would involve an unacceptable risk to innocent civilians. The emphasis is therefore being placed on political measures designed to separate the IRA from the bulk of the civilian population. The Army is adopting what is known in American jargon as a 'low profile'. How long this can continue is a matter for speculation.

To say that there is no military solution to the problems of Ireland is to state the obvious; but it is not the same as saying that there is no military solution to the problem of organised violence. The IRA can be frustrated again as they have been in the past; but, of course, as long as the political problems persist they will never be completely or permanently eliminated.

The weakness of the IRA will always lie to a great extent in its enforced concentration on the urban areas of Belfast and Londonderry. In many ways the term urban guerrilla, which Mr Robert Moss has used as the title for his book, is a contradiction in terms, as Mr Moss himself recognises. Fidel Castro's comment that 'the city is the graveyard of revolutionaries and resources' contains more than a grain of truth. Large urban areas give government forces a built-in advantage, if only because however ruthless a terrorist may be he has to accept the fact that sooner or later a compaign which results in the indiscriminate killing and maiming of women and children will alienate the population without whose support no revolutionary organisation can survive for long. Of course, the IRA can compensate for this to some extent by the classic methods of terror and coercion. Although it is wise to treat atrocity stories, from whichever side they originate, with a certain reserve, there is clear evidence of intimidation and of brutal reprisals against informers or people unwilling to co-operate with the IRA. In the long term however, these methods are self-defeating and begin to lose their power to terrorise as soon as the balance shifts towards the security forces.

The ideal conditions for guerrilla operations—mountains, jungles or broken countryside—are always likely to be denied to the IRA. They have at present a safe refuge in the Republic which enables them to carry out isolated acts of terrorism on or near the border without much risk of opposition or capture; and it will continue to exist until the government of the Republic takes more drastic action against the IRA than they have so far felt able to contemplate. In parenthesis, it should be said that the attitude of the Republic is crucial to the resolution of the present crisis, but that their situation has obvious political complications. Mr Lynch has to balance his treatment of the terrorists against the dangers to his own political survival; and if he were to disappear from the scene it is unlikely that anyone as moderate would take his place. But the operations across the border—as unpleasant and frustrating as they may be—are relatively unimportant in the context of the overall military balance. The IRA know that they cannot dominate the countryside of Northern Ireland and they will usually be restricted to striking at targets of opportunity near the border, and into conducting their main operations in Belfast and Londonderry.

At this stage it is appropriate to consider the methods which the Army employs to contain and defeat this urban threat. The first point to be made is that they have been forced, by the obvious and understandable limitations of the RUC, into tactics which are alien to the whole concept of military operations in aid of the civil power. The classic method is to hold military forces in reserve until the police are no longer able to control the situation; then to deploy troops quickly and decisively, using the minimum force, but enough of it, to restore order; and then as soon as possible to withdraw the armed forces, handing over again to the civil power. In Belfast and Londonderry the Army is, in effect, undertaking the role of the police—providing a presence in the streets, patrolling and making arrests—while at the same time being prepared to transform itself into a conventionally military force for operations against armed terrorists. In all this they are required, rightly, to operate under the severest restrictions of the common law. Each soldier carries a small yellow card setting out the restrictions to which he is subject. The card enshrines the principle of minimum force and, among other things, forbids the soldier to open fire except in cases in which a person is seen to be using a firearm, or carrying a firearm which he is about to use for offensive purposes.

The situation to which this leads is one in which soldiers, heavily armed and trained from the day of their enlistment for aggressive action, often have to stand at street corners being showered with bricks, bottles and assorted obscenities, frequently by hooligans who are little more than children. However well disciplined an Army may be—and the discipline of the British Army in Northern Ireland is of a remarkably high standard—sooner or later the fragile façade is bound to crack and someone gets killed. This is clearly what happened in Londonderry on 30 January, as the Widgery Report has now made clear beyond doubt. When the IRA use the mobs as shelter for ambushes and snipers, sooner or later a tragedy of that sort is inevitable. When it happens another weapon in the armoury of terrorism comes into its own—the weapon of propaganda. The action of the security forces in Londonderry was the subject of unceasing IRA propaganda both before and after the Widgery Report was published, and much of it was swallowed whole in sections of the British press. The violent rhetoric of revolution is a commonplace of modern life. Mr Robert Moss has quoted in his *Urban Guerrillas* a particularly obscene example of it, from the 'literature' of the Black Panthers; and on a slightly less apocalyptic, but equally vicious note the *Mini-Manual of the Irish Guerrilla*, copied almost entirely from a South American pamphlet, contains a characteristic attack on the Catholic priesthood:

> Acknowledge then the enemy in our midst, the vipers nourished by the fruits of our sweat, the black beetles eating away at our very sustenance. . . .

The fact that all this is expressed in the dense, almost illiterate jargon of political extremism should not be allowed to conceal its dangers. Combined with carefully rehearsed stories of atrocity and brutality by the security forces—usually concentrated on some particular unit or even some individual soldier—it can have a cumulative effect, not only on the Catholics of Ireland, but on the rest of the world. In the Peking *People's Daily* of the 8 February 1972 the following passage appeared in all its predictable banality:

> Of late, the people of Northern Ireland have waged a massive struggle for the democratic rights. The British Government, however, resorted to armed oppression, resulting in serious bloodshed. The incident has aroused profound indignation among all peoples of the world, the British people included. We, the Chinese people, pledge firm support for the just struggle of the Northern Irish people.

Although it may be some time before we see the Red Guards in the streets of Londonderry, and a direct confrontation between the little red book and the little yellow card, it seems clear that it is not only in the American Senate that IRA propaganda is having some success abroad. The situation is not helped, of course, by occasional excesses on the part of the government and its security forces. It is difficult to justify, on any terms, the use of interrogation methods such as those referred to by Lord Gardiner in the minority report of the Parker Committee; nor is it easy to understand that remarkable sentence in the majority report which reads in part:

`. . . we have come to the conclusion that there is no reason to rule out these techniques on moral grounds, and that it is possible to operate them in a manner consistent with the highest standard of our society.

There is scarcely any need for the IRA to invent propaganda when they are presented with gifts like that.

Generally speaking, however, the security forces in Northern Ireland are highly disciplined and tolerant even in the face of persistent provocation, and it is possible to conclude that although by force of circumstances they operate in a police role to which they are not suited by organisation or training, they are capable of containing the activities of the IRA at a level of sporadic urban terrorism which, *on its own*, would not bring about a failure of will in the British government. It is at this stage in the analysis, however, that the other factors in the balance of forces have to be taken into account. Whatever may be the patience and restraint of the government and its security forces, the attitude of the Protestant majority in Ulster is a less predictable element in the equation. It is arguable that the famous 'Protestant backlash' is now as immediate a danger as some commentators have suggested. Vanguard, the most militant group in the Protestant community, is beginning to attract wide popular support; and it would be foolish to ignore the danger of open civil war in Ulster—as in all military appreciations it is not only intentions, but capabilities as well that have to be calculated. Of a dozen or more Protestant organisations now in existence, three have a formidable potential in any clash with the IRA. The Orange Order, a worldwide organisation, is estimated to have 100,000 members in Northern Ireland alone; the Ulster Special Constabulary Association (the old 'B' Specials wearing their demob suits) have at times claimed a membership of 20,000 but are probably in effect much smaller; and there are 85 registered Rifle Clubs, with a membership of about 2,500, drawing members from the RUC, and USCA, cadets, businessmen and other enthusiasts from all over Ulster. If these organisations took to communal violence, there would be bloodshed on a scale surpassing anything Ireland has yet experienced; and the IRA would find an enemy less inhibited by the common law than the British Army, and a situation might rapidly develop in which the Army's main task would be to defend the Catholic population against the avenging Protestants. In the hands of private citizens in Ulster there are over 100,000 weapons held on certificates and permits. At Appendix B is a list of the weapons held in March 1971, and there is nothing to suggest that the situation has altered significantly since then. Although most of the weapons are shotguns, it will be seen that there are more than 1,000 high-velocity rifles and 4,500 revolvers and pistols—and most of their owners know how to use them.

Finally, in any purely military analysis, it is necessary to consider the remote but real possibility that if the Protestants decided to meet force with force there might be a kind of military intervention from the South. Although this would almost certainly be of an 'unofficial' kind in its early stages, it might conceivably bring the security forces of the Republic of Ireland into the picture. In this context it is enough to point out that the total strength of the Army of the Republic, including first line reserves, is between 10,000 and 11,000 and that most of its units are seriously under strength.

In conclusion, therefore, the following seem to be the main significant elements in the military balance affecting Northern Ireland. The Provisional IRA are still openly engaged in an attempt, through urban terrorism and the dislocation of normal life in Ulster, to overthrow the existing political order. The British Army is certainly capable of defeating this attempt, but only at the cost of persistent sporadic violence which might provoke the Protestant community into violent counter-action, leading to civil war and conceivably even into armed conflict in which the forces of the Republic of Ireland were involved. By any calculation the purely military balance lies decisively with the British government; There is virtually no combination of forces in Ireland which could inflict defeat on the Army—especially if the government were prepared, as it might need to be, to withdraw further substantial forces from the British Army of the Rhine. But this, it need hardly be said, is not a matter which can be left at that. Apart from the constant strain on its own military resources and on the patience of the British public, the government cannot contemplate an endless situation of recurrent terrorism and organised violence in the UK—however sporadic it might be in its manifestations. Besides, there are real political grievances which must be redressed; and to return to the text upon which this paper is based, no political system will survive, or even deserves to, unless it is prepared to satisfy legitimate demands for reform. In a liberal democracy this is not a matter which the politicians can leave to the soldiers; but any attempt to achieve a political solution before the rule of law is effectively restored is likely to end in failure.

TABLE OF ARMS AND EXPLOSIVES DISCOVERED BY SECURITY FORCES BEFORE AND AFTER INTERNMENT

Equipment	1 January to 8 August	9 August to 31 December
Machine guns	1	25
Rifles	66	178
Pistols/revolvers	86	158
Shotguns	40	52
Rockets	—	55
Ammunition	41,000 rounds	115,000 rounds
Explosives	1,194 lb	2,541 lb

FIREARMS IN NORTHERN IRELAND
AS AT MARCH 1971

1. Firearms held on *Certificates*:

Small-bore rifles	..	..	..	..	.. 26,100
·303 rifles	..	..	..	..	.. 680
Shotguns	..	..	..	..	.. 68,500
Revolvers/pistols	..	..	..	..	.. 3,500
Weapons not categorised	..	..	..	..	650
					99,380

2. Firearms held on *Permits*:

Small-bore rifles	..	..	..	..	.. 280
·303 rifles	..	..	..	..	.. 450
Shotguns	..	..	..	..	.. 600
Revolvers/pistols	..	..	..	..	.. 950
Weapons not categorised	..	..	..	..	410
					2,690

BIBLIOGRAPHY AND REFERENCES

Books and Official Publications

Robert Moss, *Urban Guerrillas*, Temple Smith, 1972.

Frank Kitson, *Low Intensity Operations*, Faber & Faber, 1971.

Adam Roberts (Ed), *Civilian Defence*, Faber & Faber, 1967.

W. T. Jones, *Masters of Political Thought* (Vol. II), Harrap, 1967.

Iain Hamilton, *The Irish Tangle*, Institute for the Study of Conflict, 1970.

Robert Moss, *Urban Guerrilla Warfare* (Adelphi Paper No. 79), International Institute for Strategic Studies, 1971.

The Insight Team, *Ulster*, Deutsch and Penguin, 1972.

George Grivas, *Guerrilla Warfare, Eoka's Struggle*, Longmans, 1969.

Report of the Committee of Privy Councillors (Cmnd. 4901), H.M.S.O., 1972.

Articles, etc.

Richard Middleton, 'Urban Guerilla Warfare and the IRA', *Journal of the Royal United Services Institute for Defence Studies*, December 1971.

John Whale, *Easy Consciences in Dublin*, Sunday Times, 27 February 1972.

Ian Greig, *The War over the Water*, East West Digest, March 1972.

Alun Chalfont, *The Times*, 25 January 1972.

Alun Chalfont, *Guardian*, 6 March 1972.

Ireland in the Context of the European Community

Garret FitzGerald

Ireland is sometimes seen by the British as a land of paradoxes. To the extent that this is true it reflects in some measure the multiplicity of often mutually conflicting influences to which Ireland has been subject, largely as a result of its long and complex association with Britain.

First of all Ireland is at one and the same time an ancient nation—no other culture in Europe has as long a written and oral tradition in a virtually unchanged language as has Ireland—and a recently liberated colony. Its relationship with Britain has been one of more or less continuous hostility for centuries, yet the social relationship between the two peoples is more intimate than virtually any other international relationship in the world. The home language of all but a tiny proportion of Irish people is English, but its culture is almost as different from British culture as would be possible for two nations so closely juxtaposed. Again the majority of the Irish people belong to a staunch and deeply conservative Roman Catholic tradition—yet the inspiration of its revolutionary movements for almost two centuries has been the republican tradition launched by the French Revolution. Again though Ireland has never been a colonial power—by no fault of its own, perhaps!—through the emigration of its people it has links with the word beyond the shores of Europe more enduring than those that connect many other European countries with their former colonies.

While history has left a residue of anglophobia amongst the Irish, it has also endowed Ireland with a set of political, judicial, administrative and social institutions modelled extraordinarily closely on those of Great Britain. Although the jurisdiction of the Irish State does not extend to six of Ireland's counties, almost all its other institutions—the churches, the trade union movement, the banking system, and most sporting organisations—are organised on an all-Ireland basis, totally disregarding the political division of the island!

Finally, because the Irish state founded in 1922 was in-complete, excluding the Northern Ulster Scots Protestant tradition, it has evolved in a lop-sided manner that has notably failed to reflect the whole of the island's culture and history.

Against such a complex background, fertile in paradox and anomaly, it would be too much to expect Irish attitudes and policies to have the clear-cut character manifested by those of nation-states with long, undisturbed traditions of national independence and unity, such as France and Spain—or even Germany and Italy whose political unity is of relatively recent origin, achieved only some decades before Ireland lost its historic unity as an organised society. In domestic matters these uniquely diverse historical influences have not stood in the way of the emergence of a fairly coherent approach to policy-making, however incompletely those policies reflect the complex traditions of the whole island of Ireland. But in ex-ternal policies the schizophrenia induced by such a diverse set of historical influences, finds freer rein.

Ireland's attitudes to Britain and the rest of the world are compounded of elements hard to reconcile, and the develop-ment of the Irish state during the first half-century of political independence did not require a thorough reconciliation of these elements to be effected. For the first half of this period the Irish state was preoccupied with securing an evolution from the status of a self-governing but not completely independent Dominion of the British Commonwealth to that of a sovereign Republic outside this Commonwealth. And for the second quarter-century the new Republic seemed content to opt out of foreign relationships, and to coast along without feeling any need to reconcile patent contradictions. Thus today Ireland is pulled towards Britain by close and indeed intimate ties, possibly unparalleled between independent states, and simul-taneously aroused against Britain by the conflict over the future of Northern Ireland. It is influenced by a half-century of being inward-looking, to remain aloof from international entanglements, and is pulled by its economic interests, and perhaps a lingering recollection of long-past alliances against English power, to join in a European Community to which Britain is adhering. Its successful neutrality in the last war, influenced it to opt out of the North Atlantic Alliance and has left an enduring suspicion of joint defence arrangements with other countries—and yet for religious and socio-economic reasons Ireland is one of the most fiercely anti-Communist countries in Western Europe and, because of past emigration to the United States, is also one of the most American-orientated.

One may fairly pity an Irish foreign minister trying to devise a national foreign policy that will have due regard to all these divergent influences and traditions—and yet have some internal consistency!

What constant factors can be found in Irish foreign policy over the decades? First, Irish governments have maintained friendly relations with Britain despite the irredentist passions aroused by partition. It has been a firm principle of Irish foreign policy never to allow Ireland to become, through an alliance with another power, a threat to Britain's flank. Neutrality was forced on Ireland during the second world war by the very real danger that a policy of military alignment with Western Allies would have provoked a recurrence of the Civil War that had ended only sixteen years before Hitler launched his attack on Poland. But this neutrality was firmly orientated towards Britain. Thus the Irish and British armies had secret liaison arrangements, and British aircraft were permitted to fly through Irish airspace to patrol the Atlantic. Links between the IRA and the Germans were the object of constant vigilance by the Irish security forces, and IRA activists were interned without trial for the duration of the war. The temptation to do a deal with an apparently dominant Germany with a view to securing at potentially victorious German hands a reunited Ireland was resisted, even at Britain's weakest moments. And no obstacle was placed in the way of participation in the British forces by tens of thousands of Irish men and women.

Secondly, the 'success' of neutrality in that war has profoundly influenced Irish foreign policy ever since. Ireland refused to join NATO in 1949 on the doubtful grounds that Article 4 of the Treaty involved a commitment to defend the frontiers of member states—including the frontier between Northern Ireland and the independent Irish state. This policy was accepted with enthusiasm by a strongly anti-Communist people because it represented a continuation of war-time neutrality in a new context.

Thirdly, and paradoxically, this military neutrality was accompanied by a clear-cut Cold War stance, and firm support for the Western European position *vis-à-vis* the Soviet Union. Ireland was never emotionally neutral during the Cold War—only militarily neutral.

Finally, as the country that had fought what was perhaps the first successful anti-colonial war, Ireland's sympathies have always been with the countries of Africa and Asia, and against the European colonial powers. At the same time the official expression of this sympathy has at times—especially during the 1960's—been somewhat muted in the interest of good relations with countries like Britain and France.

Throughout, Irish policies have been influenced by the partition issue—in more complex ways, perhaps, than people in Britain have realised. At one level the persistence of the division of Ireland has been a major grievance against Britain, the country which initiated this Partition in 1920, and which until 1969 supported an illiberal regime in the part of Ireland that remained within the United Kingdom. Anglo-Irish relations could never be entirely happy so long as this situation persisted.

Yet, paradoxically, partition kept Ireland close to Britain—for any radical change in the Republic, in currency, in standard time, in trade union organisation, for example, would not alone have divided the Republic from Britain (which some Irish people would have found not only tolerable but even desirable!) but also from Northern Ireland. If Britain had wished in 1920 to ensure that the new Irish state would not follow too divergent a course in these matters, it would have done what it did—partitioned the neighbouring island. No one, of course, believes that the British government at the time had any such Machiavellian intention—although many Irish people *do* believe that in partitioning Ireland the British government of the day was influenced by a desire to retain a secure military and naval base in one part of the country at least.

It does not appear that Irish governments during the early

decades of political independence understood how fundamental
to the country's interests was its continuing economic dependence on Britain. Even when Irish foreign policy was influenced,
as it surely was at times, by inhibitions arising from this dependent economic relationship, it is not clear that the limiting
effects of these inhibitions were fully appreciated. Even when
the dependent relationship, of its very nature unsatisfactory
as between two states of such disparate size, population and
economic strength, was changed to Ireland's disadvantage
over two decades ago by the introduction of the British agriculture deficiency payment scheme, few Irish people seem to
have grasped the full significance of this development: Britain's
traditional 'cheap food' policy, clearly exploitatory so far as
its food-supplying trading partners were concerned, was
thereby freed of the only inhibition that had hitherto protected
Ireland from its ravages—viz, the impact of this policy on the
British farmer. Thereafter, during the 1950's and most of the
1960's Ireland's economic growth was stunted by the deva-
stating impact of this policy upon an agricultural economy
uniquely dependent, for geographical and historical reasons, on
the British market.

Looking back, it is hard to see why the significance of this
phenomenon was not more fully grasped in Ireland; possibly
the paucity of economic talent—with several outstanding
exceptions—in the Irish governments of those years, and a
somewhat euphoric post-liberation view of the benefits of
purely political independence, may have stood in the way of a
clearer domestic view of the Irish predicament. More recently
this aspect of Ireland's politico-economic situation has become
much better understood, and the case for Irish membership of
the European Economic Community has been partly based on
the advantages to be secured by an ending of this dependent
relationship. The loss by Britain of its power to discriminate
in favour of its own farmers and against those of Ireland is
from an Irish point of view the key factor in British and Irish
membership of the Community—and the Republic can gladly
accept the loss of *its* power to 'exploit' Britain through discriminatory tariffs and quotas, as a small price to be paid for
the ending of British exploitation of Irish agriculture. It may

be noted that it is this feature of EEC membership, rather than any expectation of a major or sudden diversification of Irish exports to Western Europe, that is seen as economically and politically important in Ireland.

Against this longer-term background the present unhappy state of Anglo-Irish relations can be seen as an aberration. An almost total—and unprecedented—failure of communications between the two countries, especially after the Derry shootings, created a momentary mutual hostility that is uncharacteristic of their normal complex but basically friendly relationship with each other. That this could have happened in the face of the means of mass communications now available is astonishing and indeed deeply worrying. Past experience suggests, however, that in time the misunderstandings caused by such communications blockages will be dissipated.

The momentary hostility between Ireland and Britain has had international repercussions. The two countries' future partners in the European Community are clearly unhappy that two applicants should find themselves at loggerheads at the very moment that they are approaching entry to the Community. To the extent that this leads any of these countries to use their influence towards a peaceful solution of the Northern Ireland problem, this could prove useful.

But what of future Irish foreign policy? Where will Ireland stand within a European Community, all the other members of which are partners in the North Atlantic Alliance—although France of course no longer participates in NATO? An important influence on Irish foreign policy within the Community will be the pressure of Irish public opinion against defence commitments and in favour of the maintenance of military neutrality. To suggest otherwise would be to mislead. The campaign for membership of the Community faced a well-orchestrated counter-offensive, led by the Labour Party but largely organised by left-wing and republican elements, which placed much of its emphasis on the dangers to Irish sovereignty, and above all to Irish neutrality, arising from membership of the Community. In rebutting this thesis the proponents of membership emphasised the economic character of the Community in its present form, the need for unanimous agreement on any evolution towards a common foreign policy or defence policy, and the right of Ireland to maintain its military neutrality within the Community. This latter point has also been echoed by the French Foreign Minister, Mr. Maurice Schumann, during a visit to Ireland towards the end of 1971.

Irish supporters of EEC membership have no more enthusiasm for Irish membership of NATO than have opponents of entry to the European Community. There is in fact no support whatever in Ireland for Irish participation in NATO, or WEU. One Irish viewpoint would be that NATO is an extra-Community institution, involving politically unattractive defence links with undemocratic European countries such as Portugal and Greece, as well as a defence link with countries outside Europe that is not easily compatible with the idea of an independent Europe which is inherent in the thinking behind the EEC. The Irish and French positions have something in common on this point.

At the London meeting of the European Parliamentary Council of the European Movement in February 1971 the Irish delegation took a very active part in the organisation of opposition to British (and French) proposals to establish a foreign policy secretariat outside the Community framework. The Irish viewpoint (and Ireland had the support of Italy, the Benelux countries and Denmark on this point) was that a secretariat so situated would inevitably be the creature of governments, and that any such body should instead be set up firmly within the Community context, under the control of Community institutions in which the smaller countries have a powerful voice, and where countries like Britain and France cannot so easily force their views.

It seems likely that Ireland will pursue a policy along these lines after entry to the Community. A possible Irish line of argument would be that while the participation of most member countries of the Community in an organisation such as NATO should continue pending the development of an agreed Community foreign policy, there could be no direct link between the enlarged Community and NATO. The Community, should seek internal agreement on a common foreign policy which, hopefully, would involve a *détente* with Eastern

Europe that would in time render NATO obsolete, and bring hope of a gradual de-escalation of military forces in Europe, as well as a better relationship with the Afro-Asian countries. Any future defence commitments, to be agreed unanimously amongst the members of the Community, should be based on such an agreed foreign policy. An approach along these lines would in the Irish view be fully compatible with the principles upon which the Community is founded.

Such a viewpoint may not commend itself, however, to some members of the Community who are also members of the North Atlantic Alliance and of NATO. The fact that hitherto all the members of the Community have in fact been members of the Alliance and members or—in the case of France— an ex-member of NATO, has led to a tendency to identify the two quite different sets of international arrangements. Some German Christian Democrat and British leaders—and even some Frenchmen—seem to have difficulty in dissociating the EEC and NATO from each other, tending to talk loosely, for example, of Portugal as 'our ally', without any very clear concept of the body to which the first person plural pronoun applies. This lack of clarity will not commend itself to the Irish! It may be doubted whether some of the member countries and applicant members of the EEC have fully appreciated the significance of having a militarily neutral partner in the Community.

Membership of the enlarged Community will bring Ireland into a new relationship with its European neighbours—one which will drastically modify the somewhat bi-polarised relationship with Britain that has dominated Irish foreign policy for fifty years. Within the Community Ireland will, of course, find different allies on different subjects. To the extent that any issues divide the smaller countries from the large, Ireland with Denmark, Norway, the Netherlands and Belgium (a group with 13% of the Community's population) will—even without Luxembourg!—have power to block a decision requiring a qualified majority, if and when French objections to this voting system relent sufficiently to permit it to come into operation. On some matters of agricultural policy Ireland, France, Denmark and perhaps the Netherlands may have a similar interest—and again a power to block decisions inimical to their interests. On regional policy Ireland, Italy, France and Norway may find an identity of interest. On issues of foreign policy, where at this stage at any rate unanimity will be required for any joint decision, some Irish viewpoints may find support from Danes or Norwegians, and perhaps from the Italians, who have been advocates of a European Security Conference.

This world of shifting alliances will test Irish diplomacy to the full. Since the days of Ireland's participation in the evolution of the Dominions towards full sovereignty (1926–31), the period of the economic war with Britain culminating in the advantageous Anglo-Irish Agreement of 1938, and the wartime period when a policy of neutrality was pursued with skill and success, the Republic's abilities in this field have not really been stretched. Neither membership of the United Nations, nor participation in the Council of Europe, nor the negotiations for EEC entry—whose outcome was largely predetermined by the provisions of the Rome Treaty—have required or been the occasion for the demonstration of special diplomatic skills by Ireland. Much more will be called for, at both the diplomatic and the technical level, by membership of the Community, and the ability of a country of three million people to field a strong enough team at home and abroad, while providing its complement of officials for the European Commission and other Community institutions, must remain somewhat uncertain until tested by events.

It is against this background that the problem of Northern Ireland must be considered. The Northern Ireland situation has reached a critical stage at the very moment when Ireland and Britain are about to join the EEC. At this stage of its development the Community is directly concerned with economic matters only. Nevertheless it has been seeking to evolve common positions on foreign policy, at meetings which now comprise the foreign ministers of all ten countries. A Summit Meeting of heads of government is planned for later this year to discuss matters of common concern, and to consider the future evolution of the Community. A European Security Conference is in the offing.

The conflict in Northern Ireland is an embarrassment to all concerned at such a moment. It is embarrassing for Ireland because of the image of the country and its people being portrayed abroad as a result of the violence in Northern Ireland is one of brutality and religious intolerance. It is embarrassing for the UK Government because the British Army's role in Northern Ireland is seen by many people on the Continent as semi-colonial, and events like Derry, and those that give rise to the Compton and Parker reports, and are now before the European Commission on Human Rights, reflect very badly on Britain. And for the Community itself it is embarrassing to be faced with the adherence of two countries which appear so divided, and even at times mutually hostile, in relation to an area that seems to be disputed between them.

In these circumstances it is not surprising that some EEC governments expressed concern about the situation to the UK government long before Derry, nor would it be surprising if these communications had had some impact on the UK government. The Irish government has also shown itself sensitive to reactions abroad, modifying its post-Derry line fairly quickly in the light of reactions in certain capitals to the burning of the British Embassy in Dublin. The extent to which the embarrassments of this situation, and concern with adverse reactions in EEC countries, is at present influencing the UK government towards seeking actively a solution to the Northern Ireland problem, cannot readily be assessed at this stage. It is worth recording, however, that informed opinion in Dublin looks to pressure from EEC sources on the UK government as potentially the most hopeful external source of assistance towards a solution, the United States being written off as largely irrelevant in view of its evident reluctance to get involved in any new issues at this time; its election year preoccupations which dictate that the Northern Ireland issue be used as an election gimmick rather than be looked at as a problem in its own right; its concern to preserve close relations with the UK; and its current air transport landing rights dispute with the Irish government.

There has been some speculation in Ireland that a further deterioration in the situation in Northern Ireland and/or between the Republic and Northern Ireland, could lead to questions being raised within the EEC as to the timeliness of adherence by these two countries to the Community, but there is little evidence from the Continent itself that this is a serious issue at this stage, although one cannot exclude the possibility that it might become so.

The only overt indication of the Community's attitude towards the problem of Northern Ireland has, however, been the reply given by Professor Ralf Dahrendorf, Commissioner for External Relations, in the course of an interview with *Europaische Gemeinschaft* in April 1972, to a question as to whether history does not pose many obstacles to European unification, as exemplified by the events of Londonderry. Professor Dahrendorf replied that the example of Londonderry was an important one; the participation of Great Britain and Ireland in the Community would not solve the Irish problem, but it would diminish its intensity. In progressively adopting a common position on many problems not directly connected with the question of Northern Ireland, the differences between Great Britain and Ireland would come to be seen in a new perspective, and this would help them to resolve their specific differences over Northern Ireland. He added that friendly relations between France and Germany would have been much more difficult to preserve if they had not been members of the Community.

A quite separate issue is that of the significance of Northern Ireland to NATO. The UK troop commitment in Northern Ireland, though small in terms of the total strength of the British Army, represents a source of strain in view of the overstretched character of this Army. There have been evident difficulties in juggling troops around to provide adequate forces in Northern Ireland without denuding other areas. Moreover the possibility cannot be excluded that a deterioration in the situation in Northern Ireland might require far larger forces than are currently committed there. The present force of 15,000 men does not appear adequate to cope with such situations as renewed inter-community rioting and even warfare in Belfast; a dispersed Protestant backlash involving widespread attacks on isolated Catholics throughout the rural areas of the province; or, worst of all, an attempt by Protestant groups to achieve by military force a UDI, possibly with the support of some elements in the UDR and RUC. The danger that substantial British forces might have to be committed to prevent large-scale massacres in the North must be present to the minds of NATO planners. Moreover even the present scale of commitment, together with the danger of a larger troop involvement, must, if maintained indefinitely, raise serious problems; this may well be a source of pressure on the UK government to find a solution to the present deadlock for the NATO planners cannot be happy about the prospect of an indefinite and incalculable diversion of British land forces from Germany to Northern Ireland. They must also be concerned lest a deterioration in the situation within Ireland, and especially between the governments of Great Britain and Ireland, might provide an opportunity for non-NATO powers to dabble in troubled waters.

The risk of a confrontation with Protestant elements, possibly attempting a UDI, and with backing perhaps from some RUC and UDR elements, also carries with it the unpalatable risk of a serious deterioration in the morale of the British Army. No British government can be entirely unmindful of the 'Curragh Mutiny' and while the situation today is very different from then, the risk of a situation in which British troops might refuse to fire on their allies of yesterday cannot be totally ignored—with all that this would imply for democracy in Britain itself.

What of the military situation in the Republic? Its tiny army of 7,000 men has a very limited mobile force at its command, a fraction of which still remains in Cyprus despite a partial withdrawal brought about by the need to strengthen forces at home. This mobile force is totally inadequate for extensive border patrolling—it would find it hard to put more than a couple of men per mile along the border—and is indeed very small even to cope with the problem of internal security, especially as the police force, unlike that of Northern Ireland, has, since its foundation during the Civil War period in 1922, been unarmed, as in Britain. The armed forces of the Republic certainly constitute no threat to Northern Ireland, and their ability to intervene effectively even if requested by the UK to do so in border areas like Derry or Newry in a 'doomsday' situation beyond the British Army's control, would be very limited.

Are there any circumstances in which the Community countries could play a direct role in the Northern Ireland situation? At present it is difficult to visualise this happening, in view of Britain's firm control of the situation in Northern Ireland at this stage. Moreover Britain has made clear its determination to continue to treat Northern Ireland at least theoretically as a domestic problem, although one in which the Republic of Ireland is recognised as having an interest, of which Britain takes account by means of consultations such as those that have already taken place between the Premiers of the two countries. A serious deterioration of the situation, over-straining British military resources, and leading to a civil war type situation in Ireland, could conceivably lead to a reconsideration of this position by the UK, however. But this is still a remote contingency.

Leaving on one side the vexed question of how the present impasse in relations between the Republic, Northern Ireland and Britain can best be resolved, it may be worth considering for a moment some aspects of Community membership which have attracted little attention even in Ireland. First of all the over-weighting of the Republic's representation in the Community institutions in relation to population is necessarily accompanied by a corresponding although not proportionate under-weighting of larger countries such as the UK. The net effect of this is that, for example, in the European Parliament Northern Ireland, if it gets its fair share ($2\frac{3}{4}\%$) of UK representation, will have one member—whereas the Republic, with a national output little more than 50% greater and a population just twice as large, will have ten members!

Again, the Republic will nominate one member of the Commission; Northern Ireland, unless by an improbable chance a resident of that area is selected as one of the UK's two Commissioners, will have no representation at that level in the Commission and, one suspects, a much smaller ratio of other Commission posts than its size relationship with the Republic might seem to justify. Finally, in the Council of

Ministers the UK's ten votes are to be cast *en bloc* by the UK minister attending any particular meeting, and they will certainly be used in the interests of the UK as a whole rather than in the interest of Northern Ireland should a clash of interest occur between the two—as may well arise on a number of issues.

What this adds up to is a very unsatisfactory situation from the point of view of Northern Ireland, which, because its economic interests within an enlarged Community will frequently correspond more closely to those of the Republic than to those of the UK, may well find itself in the somewhat invidious position of being better represented by its Irish neighbours than by its British rulers. Arguably the interests of Northern Ireland within the Community, on such matters as agricultural and regional policy, for example, would be better served within a united Ireland (where, incidentally, it might benefit from the Republic's export tax relief concession), than within the UK.

Membership of the Community by the United Kingdom and the Republic will have other effects so far as Northern Ireland is concerned. For one thing it will eliminate the divergence between farm prices North and South of the Border which must at present provide a potent economic argument, even for Catholic farmers in Northern Ireland, against the reunification of Ireland. Participation together in the work of European institutions is also likely to enhance the sense of a common Irish identity which at present finds its most vocal and lively expression when Ireland plays England in Rugby football!

There is also the question of Community regional policy. The Commission has a special interest in regional policy problems that arise in frontier situations; it is already involved in helping to plan as a unit the development of the region comprising parts of south-east Holland, north-east Belgium, and Germany west of the Ruhr, and some Commission officials have expressed an interest in helping with the regional problems created by the Irish border, e.g. between Derry and Donegal, and within the Fermanagh/Cavan/Leitrim area—perhaps the poorest part of Ireland, which suffers additionally from the border division. The problem of regional development in these areas which is complicated by the Border and by

Northern Ireland government sensitivities about initiatives from the Republic in connection with the joint development of the region, could be tackled effectively under Commission auspices—and perhaps only in this way.

A feature of Northern Ireland legislation which has affected its relations with the Republic has been the Safeguarding of Employment Act, passed after the last war, which is designed to restrict employment in the region to residents of Northern Ireland. While this legislation is not expressly discriminatory *vis-à-vis* residents of the Republic, and while there have been cases of residents of Great Britain being refused employment permits, it has been construed in the Republic as an attempt to prevent the immigration into Northern Ireland of Catholics from the Republic, rather than as being purely a measure to deal with local unemployment. A derogation from the provisions of the Rome Treaty with respect to free movement of workers has been granted for the duration of the transitional period, with provision for further discussion of the matter at the end of that period. The question of any extension of this derogation would need to be considered in the political context of the Irish situation at that time and not merely in the context of the Northern Ireland economic situation.

If the Community develops a social policy comprising a harmonisation of social security, and ultimately joint financing of social security, this would have a very important part to play in helping to resolve economic differences between North and South. At the present time Northern Ireland, whose output per head and living standards are lower than in the rest of the UK by about 20%, and whose rates of dependency and unemployment are higher than in the rest of the UK, has its social services heavily subsidised by Great Britain. Total expenditure on social welfare and health in the region is estimated at about £195 million in 1971/72, (the 1970/71 financial year figure was £184·9m.), but £72m. of this was provided by way of direct subsidy.

The Republic, lacking similar subsidisation, and with output per head and living standards about 40% below the UK level, necessarily has a much lower level of social security and health service provision. It has been estimated that it would cost the Republic £145m. to have raised these provisions to the British and Northern Ireland level in 1969/70, and the figure would be a good deal higher today. Further large sums would be required if its housing provision and educational service were also to be raised to the British and Northern Ireland level.

At the present time the only way in which one can visualise the disparity in social services on either side of the Border being overcome in the context of a United Ireland would be by means of a continued British subsidy to Northern Ireland, possibly tapering off over the remaining years of the century, by the end of which faster growth in Ireland may well have brought per capita output and living standards in the island close to the UK level. (During the 1960s the growth rate in both parts of Ireland was about 40% faster than in Britain.) If, however, the EEC, as a logical corollary to economic and monetary union and to its agricultural and regional policies, were to develop a common social security policy, this would provide an alternative, and from the British and Irish viewpoints preferable, solution to this problem. (A more detailed analysis of the Northern Ireland subsidy situation is set out in an Appendix.)

Community membership by the two countries will not of itself solve the problem of Irish unity, but as Professor Dahrendorf has said it will in significant measure assist its solution. This, indeed, is an added political reason for Irish membership, although it did not feature largely in the referendum campaign—in which, indeed, opponents of membership counter-argued somewhat unconvincingly that the Republic should not join because it would appear that most people in Northern Ireland, Catholic and Protestant alike, are opposed to membership or at best indifferent about it, and because, it was suggested, membership will fix unalterably the boundary between the two parts of Ireland.

The Ulster Debate

Robert Moss

It has probably become impossible to reach consensus on Northern Ireland. The ISC Study Group did not manage to draw up an abstract blueprint for any kind of 'final solution' for Ulster; it did attempt to define the guidelines for a political settlement to the conflict, and the obstacles to any settlement, in the understanding that there can be no purely military solution for political violence. It is obvious to everyone that it is in Britain's interests to end the conflict as quickly as possible. The need to deploy upwards of 15,000 troops in Ulster has cut into the resources of the British Army on the Rhine and so diminished the United Kingdom's contribution to NATO—although a cynic might observe that the practical experience of street-skirmishing and counter-guerrilla operations that the Army has acquired in Belfast and Londonderry may prove useful in other situations. The violence in Ulster is in some ways an embarrassment to Britain at a moment when it is about to enter the European Economic Community. It has jeopardised relations with the Dublin government and exposed Britain to a certain amount of criticism from other countries, and notably from the Irish-American lobby in the United States.

Some people would add that the fighting has added to the already considerable economic burden of subsidising the social welfare schemes and the economic development of Northern Ireland (which represents a drain on Britain's resources of some £240 million a year) and that this is a reason for pulling out of the province altogether. But Britain's interests have to be weighed against Britain's responsibilities. Whatever final settlement is found for Ulster (especially if it proves to be the unification of Ireland) it will be unlikely to lessen the financial burden for Britain in the short term. The British government has a historical responsibility to the people of Northern Ireland, and it has undertaken not to impose basic constitutional changes without the consent of the majority. At the same time, the political future of both parts of Ireland cannot be viewed with indifference from London, since a prolonged civil war or the emergence of an extremist regime in an off-shore island would directly affect Britain's security. The conflict in Ulster may appear anachronistic or irrelevant to outsiders who maintain that the central problem for the North and the South is to find ways of promoting economic growth within an enlarged EEC; but it is a reality that no British government can afford to shrug off. And the final outcome in Ulster has a broader import. If the IRA are seen to succeed in any of their major goals, that will serve to encourage political extremists farther afield, and possibly in other parts of the UK.

The Study Group met in April shortly after the British government suspended the Stormont parliament for a nominal period of twelve months and entrusted Mr William Whitelaw with responsibility for the administration of the province as Secretary of State for Northern Ireland. This 'political initiative' raised hopes of a compromise with moderate Catholic leaders that would cut the ground away from under the feet of the IRA, although it also raised fears of a violent reaction from the Protestant community. After more than two years of campaigning, the British Army had learned the limits of force in a context of Catholic alienation. But it also seemed possible that the British government was about to experience the limits of politics in a situation where an armed minority had established its hold over a significant section of the civil population.

The imposition of direct rule also created some new problems. It meant, for a start, that both the Catholics and the Protestants in Northern Ireland could hold the British government directly responsible for every event of which they happened to disapprove. It was also a godsend for Republicans who wanted to practise 'anti-colonialist' propaganda. Finally, as one member of the Study Group argued, the assumption of direct rule increased Britain's moral commitment to restore order in the province.

1. The Shape of a Political Settlement

The first task for the Study Group was to try to outline the kind of political compromise that might be viable in Northern

Ireland. It was agreed that the immediate objective should be to construct the machinery for short-term reconciliation and long-term self-determination, in the understanding that a 'final solution' for Northern Ireland can only follow many years of debate. Britain's long-term options in Ulster could be set out as follows:

(i) The restoration of some form of regional parliament or community administration;

(ii) Full integration of Northern Ireland into the UK;

(iii) Unification of the two parts of Ireland within a new federal (or confederal, with the UK) constitution;

(iv) Tolerance of a Protestant UDI that would lead to the creation of an independent state covering at least four of the six provinces of Ulster—and probably also to direct confrontation with the Republic of Ireland;

(v) An announced deadline for British withdrawal from the province that would leave it to the political forces within Northern Ireland to decide their own destiny— which would almost certainly mean bloody civil war, possibly resulting in Protestant UDI.

The last two possibilities, of course, are not really options for any responsible British policy-maker, but simply counsels of despair.

The Study Group was agreed on two basic principles. The first is that no basic decisions can be taken at this stage on the long-term political status of Northern Ireland. That can only be determined over a long period of discussion between all parties involved. At the same time, it is essential to reaffirm the guarantee that no decision will be imposed against the will of the majority in the province. The second principle is that, while it is desirable to retain some form of regional administration, it is necessary to modify the Stormont system. Most of the Study Group agreed that the Stormont parliament in its old form failed to bring Catholic politicians into the decision-making process and failed to provide a means of reconciliation between the two communities in Northern Ireland—although it is important to remember that successive Unionist governments since 1969 showed a genuine willingness to bring about social reform. It is still true that under the old system, the Protestant hegemony—and in practice, Unionist Party domination—was guaranteed. For this reason, it would seem that a form of democracy based simply on the principle of 'one man, one vote' does not allow Catholic leaders to exercise a genuine role in the administration of Ulster. Members of the Study Group suggested a number of innovations that would allow Ulster Catholics a greater measure of participation within a new 'community administration'. These included proportionate party representation in the future provincial cabinet and the substitution of a system of proportional representation in place of the present pattern of constituency voting.

One of the most imaginative suggestions concerned a revision of the method of voting within the Stormont parliament. It was suggested that to bring a fixed number of Catholic politicians into future provincial governments would not, in itself, give them a real political base or any genuine bargaining power. For this reason, Sir Frederick Catherwood proposed a new method of voting that would require a 75% majority for the passing of bills in a revised Stormont legislature. This, he contended, would force Catholic and Protestant politicians to come together on essential issues and to form a non-sectarian coalition. His ideas are set out in greater detail in his paper, printed as an appendix. But, however desirable in principle, the Catherwood proposals and other suggestions for revision of the Stormont system must be viewed in the context of the day-to-day problems of violence and sectarian hatred that any future administration in Northern Ireland will have to confront. For the moment, the situation in the province is such that no one can guarantee that the irrational will not once again triumph over rational attempts at compromise. It is also clear that any future community administration—if it is to be more than a mere talking-shop—must be able to take decisions quickly and decisively, especially if it is to have any say in the handling of security. It is questionable whether a system of parliamentary voting that required a 75% majority for the acceptance of new legislation would fulfil this criterion.

On the other hand, some members of the Study Group argued that the Catherwood system would have the dual advantage of (a) serving as an experiment in Protestant–Catholic co-operation while (b) providing a guarantee to the Protestant majority that no changes in Ulster's constitutional status would be made without their consent. If the voting requirement for routine legislation were 75%, the proportion could hardly be less for a bill involving a crucial question such as the future political status of the province.

The role of a future community administration would probably be confined—at least at the outset—to matters such as health, education and social welfare. If it received the support of both communities, it would provide an opportunity to press ahead with the reform programme already enacted by Unionist governments since 1969. If the British government, temporarily at least, retained responsibility for security, the new provincial administration could afford to experiment with a new voting system or a new method of distributing cabinet posts that might otherwise prove a stumbling-block for the prosecution of the campaign against the IRA. But there is an element of risk involved in all these suggestions, and it was even argued that, without a reasonable chance of general agreement in the near future, direct rule might merely prove 'a perilous addition to an already intolerable burden'.

It was agreed that it is vital to bring the Dublin government into any future negotiations on the constitution of Northern Ireland. The machinery for achieving this might be some form of *Council of Ireland* as a forum for government-to-government discussions. The agenda for such a council should cover the following problems:

(a) Economic co-operation

Experiments in the development of transnational economic regions within the EEC might serve as a model for a new approach to the development of border areas. It was argued, for example, that the creation of the border between North and South has in some ways 'distorted' the commerce and industry of the island as a whole. Londonderry, to take one case, would appear to be a natural distributing centre for much of County Donegal. The most pressing socio-economic problem in both parts of Ireland is unemployment, and it should be possible to draw up a list of joint development projects along the border designed to create jobs for men who are out of work on both sides. One concrete proposal was for the creation of a free port near Londonderry, although this would run into commercial opposition from the shippers of Belfast and the men in charge of the deep-sea nuclear submarine base at Holy Loch in Scotland would not welcome any substantial increase in the shipping plying to and from the west coast of Ireland.

(b) Joint planning for the EEC
It was argued that both parts of Ireland have common agricultural interests to defend within an enlarged European Economic Community.

(c) Social welfare policy
The recent improvements in the social benefits scheme in the Republic have not served to close the considerable gap between the welfare systems of North and South. Ulster's system of social benefits, which follows that of the UK, depends on British subsidies and one of the most formidable obstacles to the reunification of Ireland is the present inability of the Republic to (i) bring the social welfare system in the South up to UK standards and (ii) finance the social benefits scheme in the North that depends on British subsidies.

(d) Revision of the Irish constitution
The prospects for eventual unification of Ireland will partly depend on the capacity of the Dublin government to satisfy Northern Protestants that it is ready to abolish sectarian legislation and that there is no discrimination on the basis of religion in the South. The declining Protestant population of the Republic has not been a notable source of reassurance on this score, although this is partly due to the fact that the Catholic church requires the children of mixed marriages to be raised in the Catholic faith.

(e) Joint action against the IRA
This is discussed in the second part of this paper.

One of the advantages of a Council of Ireland working along

these lines would be that it would force those taking part to dig beneath the myths of Republicanism and take a hard look at the political, social and economic obstacles to the unification of Ireland. The figures quoted by Dr Garret FitzGerald—which reveal that at present Britain is paying out about £230–240m. in direct and indirect subsidies to Northern Ireland—show that the obstacles to unity go far beyond Protestant resistance and the reluctance of the Dublin government to revise its constitution to make the system in the South more attractive to Northern Protestants. There is also the problem of hard cash, and it is very difficult to see how the unification of Ireland would be economically viable within the next two decades without massive British subsidisation.

2. *The Security Problem*

In trying to chart the future course of events in Northern Ireland, it is necessary to distinguish what is likely to happen from what ought to happen. The strategy that Mr William Whitelaw set out to apply as Secretary of State for Northern Ireland after March 1972, was founded on the first principle of all counter-insurgency campaigning: that victory depends on isolating the rebel from his civilian supporters, on draining the water from the fish. While all members of the Study Group agreed that the British government's political initiative increased the chance of winning back the support of Catholic moderates, there was considerable divergence of opinion on the question of how far the search for political compromise should be underpinned by military action.

Some members felt that (regardless of Protestant reactions) the security forces should be kept outside the so-called no-go areas in the Catholic areas and that all internees should be released or brought to trial. They argued that, to the extent that the strength of the IRA was based upon genuine grievances and the emotions aroused by military searches and detention without trial, a softer approach would be a powerful inducement to ordinary Catholics to close their doors to the gunmen. Other members of the Study Group insisted that it was naive to overlook the capacity of the IRA as an organisation to enforce its hold over the civil population by coercive terrorism or to sabotage the British government's initiative through a continued campaign of violence. They argued that it was the responsibility of the government (while searching for compromise) to enforce the rule of law in all parts of the province.

There is reason in both arguments. It is my personal view that there are several dangers involved in the first approach. It might be characterised as the 'wither-on-the-vine' strategy. That is, the argument runs, that by suspending Stormont and opening a debate on the future constitution of Ulster, the British government has made it possible for Catholic moderates to take a stronger stand against the IRA. So long as Mr Whitelaw 'produces the goods' by releasing internees and so long as the security forces avoid incidents that could lead to serious civilian casualties (like the shootings in Londonderry on 30 January) the IRA will simply wither on the vine. The argument continues that, in order to restore Catholic confidence in the intentions of the British government, it is worth running the risk of setting hard-core terrorists at liberty, of allowing IRA units virtual sanctuary in the no-go areas, and of provoking a violent reaction from Protestant militants.

It seems to me that the success of this approach (which, some members of the Group maintained, is more or less what Mr Whitelaw has been entrusted with carrying out) would depend on three things. The first is the capacity and the desire of Catholic moderates to swing the Catholic community against the IRA. They can be helped, not merely by the release of internees or a 'softly, softly' approach by the British Army, but by development programmes designed to produce new jobs quickly. But they have to contend with the second factor, which is the entrenched position of the IRA within many of the Catholic areas. In the Bogside area of Londonderry, 200 IRA gunmen are moving amongst a population of some 25,000 people, unchecked by the security forces. The IRA and Catholic vigilante groups have established their own system of policing, with check-points and night patrols. It is in this context that the IRA are able to practise the forms of coercive terrorism familiar to rebel movements throughout history, and perfected by the National Liberation Front (FLN) in Algeria and the Vietcong in South Vietnam. The third factor is the

capacity of both Catholic and Protestant extremists to under-
mine the hope of a political settlement. It would seem to be in
the interests of both groups at this stage to provoke the kind of
communal civil war that would cast both the IRA and the
Protestant vigilantes in the archaic role of community de-
fenders.

The general point can be put simply: that it is doubtful
from historical experience whether it is possible to isolate a
terrorist organisation by purely political measures once it has
built up support in the civil population. The authorities also
have to offer *protection*. The situation in the no-go areas of
Northern Ireland after the imposition of direct rule may not
have amounted to anarchy, in the sense that local Catholic
citizens' groups showed some capacity to organise their own
para-police forces and to curb normal forms of crime. But it
was doubtful whether these 'embryonic police forces',*
organised outside the law, provided any real protection against
the coercive terrorism of both wings of the IRA, and reports
continued to stream in of the exercise of 'revolutionary
justice', ranging from tarring-and-feathering for 'criminal'
offences to the murder of informers. One particularly savage
case of IRA intimidation was the murder of a bus driver in
January 1972, who was the key witness in the trial of two
men responsible for hijacking a bus. Against this background, it would seem to be short-sighted to discuss how to
win 'hearts and minds' without also considering how to protect bodies.

The Study Group's discussions of the problem of confronting
the IRA as a military organisation centred on four main issues:
IRA activity south of the border; the legal framework for
counter-guerrilla operations; the problem of policing; and the
use of regular troops in built-up areas.

(i) The Border Problem
Some members felt that there is no hope of suppressing the IRA
without sealing off its sanctuaries in the Republic. This would
mean either (a) closing the border or (b) enlisting the active

---

* John Graham in the *Financial Times*, 12 April 1972.

support of the Irish government. Most members of the Study Group agreed that (a) was impracticable, although one member argued that recent American experiments in electronics (including the development of new types of sensors) have made the project technically feasible. At the same time, it was agreed that past attempts at limiting the movement of gunmen across the border by cratering roads and setting up check-points have been hopelessly inadequate, for legal as well as technical reasons. For example, civil law does not permit the security forces to crater private roads, nor to stop private individuals from filling up holes in public roads as soon as they have been engineered. It was suggested that—through the deployment of more troops and the setting-up of more obstacles like electrified fences—it would be practicable at least to block off favourite access-points for the IRA along the border near Londonderry.

But the movement of gunmen across the border can probably only be curbed effectively with the co-operation of the Dublin government. The limited manpower and even more limited mobility of the Irish security forces (the recall of eight armoured cars from Cyprus in October 1971 brought the grand total to sixteen) would make thorough policing of the southern side of the border difficult even if the government in Dublin had the political will to undertake it. It has been claimed that there are four counties of Ireland where the Army is already virtually operating in hostile territory, and where units are issued with gas-masks before they arrive on tours of duty. But it is the intelligence gathered by Garda Special Branch that would probably be the decisive factor. However, the British initiative in March did not immediately prompt Mr Jack Lynch to take any new measures against the IRA in the south. It was agreed that, in the present climate of opinion, the Dublin government would resort to the use of internment only in the face of the direct threat of a local uprising. But there are other legal weapons that could be used against the IRA in the Republic, notably the use of regulations providing for temporary detention or of special criminal courts to prevent the intimidation of magistrates and witnesses. The problem, as for all security forces that have to contend with armed extremists while working within the framework of civil law, is to pin down sufficient evidence to secure conviction.

The importance of the sanctuaries in the South to the IRA in the North was disputed within the Study Group, and it was pointed out that arms and supplies come from many sources (funds from American sympathisers; much of the gelignite from contacts in Wales and Scotland). There are an estimated 200 or 300 Provisionals from the North present in the Republic on 'rest and recreation'. Some have been reluctant to return, but 25–50 gunmen are available to go North at short notice on any one occasion. The IRA bases in the South were held to be more important for training and refuge than as a source of new recruits for the fighting in Ulster, and the role of Southern gunmen in the North early in 1972 was considered to be minimal.

(ii) The Legal Framework

All members of the Study Group agreed on the principle that a government confronted with urban terrorism must be able to exercise some exceptional legal powers. You cannot treat urban guerrillas in the same way as car thieves. But there was no consensus on the subject of internment. It was accepted that the introduction of internment in August 1971 had deepened the alienation of the Catholic community. But it was also suggested that the intelligence acquired through internment had enabled the security forces to locate important arms caches and to round up several hundred Provisionals and Officials after internment came into force. Thus the usefulness of internment (or, at the least, a form of temporary detention) as an instrument of the security forces has to be carefully weighed against the resentment it aroused in the Catholic population and the moral objection that it is undesirable to suspend the citizen's right to a fair trial in a functioning democracy even in conditions of internal war.

The immediate question for the British government is how many internees can be safely released as a gesture toward Catholic opinion in Ulster. Is it in fact advisable to release *all* remaining internees who cannot be brought to trial because of lack of evidence or who are found not guilty in a normal court?

The government is currently following a programme of the phased release of internees after close study of their case-files. This has the advantages of (a) presenting the Catholic community with concrete evidence of the government's willingness to seek compromise while (b) minimising the risk that hard-core elements will be turned loose in the streets before the Catholic moderate leaders have been given time to pursue serious negotiations in search of a political settlement. It was argued that the first batches of returning internees would serve as 'ambassadors' in their own community. Although it has been claimed that one Provisional officer released a fortnight after direct rule was imposed has gone back to the command of a west Belfast IRA company, the gamble involved in setting free the first few hundred internees was probably worth taking.

The real dilemma for the British government will come when it has to decide on how to handle members of the IRA known to be dangerous and committed but immune to trial because of lack of evidence. That decision must hinge upon the level of violence and the performance of those men (the John Humes and Gerry Fitt) who are still being looked to to provide a strong lead against the IRA. There was some support within the Study Group for the idea that, if the terrorist campaign has not diminished and no further progress has been made towards a political settlement over a period of several months, the policy of phased release of internees must be reconsidered. But there was also another body of opinion that maintained that the government must work towards the ending of internment as a legal weapon and confine itself to 28-day detention orders and trials *in camera*. It is my personal view that, in a situation of internal war, the security forces must be allowed the *power* to intern, but that it should be exercised with the utmost care. In a situation where witnesses are subject to intimidation, there must be some means of taking known gunmen off the streets. To minimise the public hostility that this is bound to arouse in some quarters, the security forces will require good intelligence and will need to follow a highly selective approach.

Perhaps the acid test for the policy adopted in March 1972

will be the track record of the men who have been released. To
the extent that they revert to violence, internment will appear
justified in retrospect and Unionist politicians as well as
Protestant extremists will appear confirmed in their criticisms
of the British government's 'soft' approach to the security
problem. To the extent that the men released eschew
violence and live peacefully among the Catholic community, a
policy of concessions will be validated. This means that it is
essential at this stage for the government to think beyond the
mere release of prisoners to the problem of *rehabilitation of
detainees*. Is a member of the IRA, returning from Long Kesh
to Bogside and finding one man in five unemployed and no
police around, likely to spend all his mornings at the labour
exchange? Even if he is that way inclined, is it not probable
that his old comrades will try to coax or compel him back into
the terrorist campaign? The men coming back from behind
the wire will require both jobs and surveillance.

(iii) The Problem of Policing

One of the heretical, but stimulating, suggestions raised within
the Study Group was that under a future community administration, the Royal Ulster Constabulary might draw on
the support of local citizens' defence associations, organised on
the model of the 'tenant aides' and 'community wardens'
active in Pittsburgh and other American cities. This would be
one way, perhaps, of solving the problem of policing the
Catholic ghettoes, where the RUC has been a declining
presence since the late 1960s. It would be one way of harnessing
the energies of the community para-police organisations
already active in areas like the Creggan and the Bogside in
Londonderry.

The danger, of course, is that to rely on these groups could
amount to the same thing as relying on the Black Panthers to
police Harlem. Although the Catholic vigilantes must be
regarded as separate from the IRA and not necessarily aligned
with it, the success of the IRA Officials in penetrating and
finally taking over the Northern Ireland Civil Rights Association (NICRA) provides a model of how the IRA can operate
to turn a broader communal movement into a front organisa-

tion.* It is arguable that to depart from the principle of a nationwide, unitary police force might amount to licensing private armies in the Protestant as well as Catholic areas. At the same time, one of the immediate problems in Ulster is how to protect the ordinary Catholic against IRA intimidation in a context of sectarian hatred and distrust of the security forces.

The Study Group was in broad agreement that, while the British Army has ample means to sweep through the no-go areas—at considerable risk to innocent civilians—this would probably destroy the hopes of a political settlement at this stage. The alternative is a low-key approach, involving highly selective arrest operations and above all close contact with Catholic community leaders opposed to the IRA.

(iv) The Army Role

One of the recurring problems for the Study Group (which met just before the publication of Lord Widgery's findings on the shootings in Londonderry on 30 January) concerned the use of regular soldiers to police urban areas. The British Army was called upon to do more in Ulster than the phrase 'operations in aid of the civil power' normally denotes; it actually had to stand in for the police in many situations where it was exposed to the constant frustration of having to respond to rioters, snipers and bombers while hedged in by many legal restraints. This was certainly a brutalising confrontation for both sides. The remarkable thing (as most members of the Study Group were ready to concede, with one or two notable exceptions) was that discipline was maintained so well, and that there were so few cases of over-reaction.

In my own view, one of the basic psychological problems for the British Army stemmed from the selective judgment of many Ulster Catholics, who seemed to show high tolerance for IRA-perpetrated atrocities but very little for normal riot-control procedures. Political extremists build on this kind of selective judgment. The *Sunday Times'* inquiry into the accuracy of the Widgery report was entitled 'The Decision to Put

* See, for example, "Derry" Kelleher's article 'The Civil Rights Take-over' in *Hibernia*, 3 March 1972.

Civilians at Risk' (a reference to the decision to send the 1st Parachute Regiment into the Bogside on an arrest operation during the illegal march on 30 January).* The IRA leaders, of course, make precisely that decision every day, when bombs are planted in city stores or snipers fire from the back of a crowd. Lord Widgery held that the initial responsibility for 'Bloody Sunday' lay with the organisers of the illegal march—the NICRA, which is controlled by the Official wing of the IRA.† The inquest into the Derry shootings illustrated the dilemmas for an outside force of regular soldiers operating in a crowded urban area where they frequently have to make the difficult choice between going 'all out for the gunmen, in which case the innocent suffer' or putting the safety of the innocent first, 'in which case many gunmen will escape and the risk to themselves will be increased'.

It is clearly undesirable in principle to use soldiers in routine police assignments. In Northern Ireland, because of the fact that the RUC had been overstretched and was discredited in the minds of many Catholics as a result of its actions in August 1969, this was unavoidable. But there are obvious problems for an outside force brought into an unfamiliar built-up area on a short term of duty. For a start, it may be difficult for soldiers unfamiliar with the local population to distinguish rioters from 'riot-containers'—moderates in the crowd attempting to persuade the others to go home. They may not have sufficient local intelligence. And they constantly have to take split-second decisions that may endanger innocent lives. Is the man at the back of the crowd holding a nail-bomb or half a brick? Is that a photographer using a telescopic lens or a terrorist pointing a submachine-gun?

But for the moment, there seems little hope of cutting back significantly on British troop levels in Northern Ireland. The RUC and the Ulster Defence Regiment are largely composed of Protestants (the proportion of Catholics is only around 11–12%) and are thus open to the charge of being 'sectarian'. Local vigilante groups cannot take the place of a force re-

* 23 April 1972.

† *Report of the Tribunal appointed to inquire into the Events of Sunday, 30 January 1972.* HMSO, 12 April 1972.

sponsible to the central government, and may merely serve as a vehicle for political extremists. Most members of the Study Group agreed that the idea of withdrawing the British Army from the urban areas to take up positions on neighbouring hills or along the border was simply unrealistic, and that the government must be ready to contemplate the deployment of a greater number of troops if the political initiative breaks down.

3. The Prospects

It is too early to pass judgment on the success of the political initiative. There were several grounds for modest optimism in the immediate aftermath of the imposition of direct rule. Some Catholic leaders in the north, notably parish priests in Belfast (crucial opinion-formers in the Catholic ghettoes), moderate politicians like Mr John Hume and ordinary housewives in areas like Andersonstown took an open stand against a continued campaign of terror. But at the same time, both wings of the IRA announced that they intended to go on with their programme of violence (although the Officials decided to call a truce in May).

The motives of the IRA leaders were clear enough. It was not just that they remained deeply suspicious of a political deal proposed by a British government, nor even that individual gunmen were worried about their job prospects if they were to lay aside their weapons and look for honest employment. The greatest fear of the IRA chiefs was that they would see the initiative taken away from them by moderate leaders. The election held for a residents' council in the Bogside area of Derry (an IRA stronghold) in April suggested that Catholic public opinion was starting to run against the terrorists, since not one of the twelve people elected was identified as a member of the IRA.

There appears to be some division between Provisional and Official tacticians over the methods they should now employ to maintain their grip over the Catholic ghettoes. Even within the Provisional wing, there is growing interest in non-violent forms of political agitation and subversion. But it was also argued that the temptation for the IRA to use coercive terrorism against their Catholic rivals and to provoke the

Protestants and the security forces through the familiar pattern of bombing and assassination will increase, rather than diminish, as a genuine peace movement among Ulster Catholics gathers support.

It is also clear that the challenge to the political initiative comes from the Protestant right as well as the IRA. The much-heralded 'Protestant backlash' did not lead to communal slaughter or counter-terrorism in the first months after direct rule was imposed, but there was a significant show of support for Mr William Craig's Vanguard movement, and late in May 10,000 members of the Ulster Defence Association paraded in military-style dress in Belfast. The general sense of suspicion and bitterness among the Protestant community will hardly make it easier for the British to achieve a settlement acceptable to all parties. It is possible to imagine a situation in which the British Army might be called upon to act against Protestant extremists.

In Northern Ireland, the British government has had to confront one of the classic dilemmas of a democratic society exposed to political violence: how much force can the society use to defend itself without departing from the legal and political traditions that the authorities are concerned to uphold? Many members of the Study Group felt that, by 'pulling the stops out', the British Army could clear the IRA out of the no-go areas and reduce the violence in the province to a 'tolerable' level—although this does not mean that they could suppress the IRA once and for all. Governments that have dealt with urban insurgencies in other countries, unburdened by moral scruples or respect for civil law, have had fairly general success. One only has to think of the methods applied by the French in Algiers or the Brazilians in São Paulo and Rio de Janeiro. But all members of the Study Group were agreed that the British government was right to accept the restraints of a functioning democracy in the confrontation with the IRA.

Most members were also agreed that the discipline of the British Army has remained extraordinarily high, and that there have been very few occasions when the Army can be shown to have deviated from the policy of 'minimal force'.

Figures cited by Lord Widgery show that between 1 August 1971 and 9 February 1972, 2,656 shots were fired at the security forces in Londonderry; 456 nail bombs and gelignite bombs were thrown at them; and there were 225 explosions in the city. In response, the security forces fired back only 840 live rounds. It is difficult to see how these figures could be used by an impartial observer to sustain the thesis that the Army has 'over-reacted'. At the same time, it is clear that the Army has to work by different rules from those accepted by the IRA. It is responsible to public opinion and to elected politicians, while the gunmen are not. All security operations in Northern Ireland have been conducted within the framework of law, and the day-to-day behaviour of the Army is subject to the regulations laid down in the 'yellow card' that each soldier has to carry.

These points are made cogently by Lord Chalfont in his paper, but they are worth stressing again because, in the last analysis, every attempt to contain political violence is an exercise in psychological warfare. The chances for a political settlement in Northern Ireland hinge on the hope that reasonable men can overcome the force of rumour and blind reaction, and that moderate leaders can overcome the terrorists' tactics of provocation and intimidation. If, by provoking a violent confrontation with the 'tartan gangs' of working-class Protestant youths and with militant Orangemen, the IRA can create the conditions for a full-scale civil war in Ulster, Mr Whitelaw's role as a conciliator will become impossible. That is why the government must have its contingency plans ready, while hoping that they will never have to be applied. The IRA's reaction to the British government's March initiative suggests that the Army will have to contend with an organised terrorist campaign for some time to come. The responsibility to reassert the rule of law cannot be shrugged off. Military action is no substitute for a political settlement, but submission to violence cannot be the basis for compromise.

Appendix I
A POSSIBLE POLITICAL SETTLEMENT
OF THE NORTHERN IRELAND
PROBLEM*

Frederick Catherwood

It is by now fairly clear that the problem of government by
consent in Northern Ireland cannot be solved by any of the
traditional political formulae. Union with the Republic
against the consent of the majority in Northern Ireland would
simply substitute a dissident minority of a million within the
Republic for a dissident minority of a half million within the
Province. Democratic voting will continue to produce a
Unionist majority for as long as the minority continue to vote
on nationalist and religious lines. Amendment of the border
does not solve the problem of the nationalists in Belfast. And
the suspension of Stormont is not at present adding to the
measure of consent with which the Province is governed.

It is necessary to set the problem out like this again only to
underline the point that the achievement of the measure of
consent normally present within a democracy requires a
different formula in Northern Ireland from those by which
democracy normally operates. The rule of the majority and
the acquiescence of the minority may be the right formula for
good government in almost every case, but that does not give
it the status of divine right. It is a pragmatic principle, found
to work in most cases, but after fifty years of one-party government in Northern Ireland it is regrettably evident that it is
no longer sufficient as a method of obtaining consent in that
Province. It may be that there is no political formula which
will produce consent, but there is one variation of democracy
which is at least worth examining, that is to raise the majority
required for the passage of legislation through the provincial
parliament.

Although in most democracies, most legislation can be

* A version of this paper was first read to members of a Chatham House
conference on Ireland in January 1972.

passed by a simple majority, there are occasions when a higher majority is required. Even in Britain, where there is no precise constitutional requirement, it was generally thought desirable that the Common Market terms should be carried by more than a bare majority. And it is generally thought undesirable that a government with a very small majority should run its full term. Second chambers and other constitutional rules are used to modify the general rule so that a bare majority in the popularly elected chamber cannot in all circumstances carry all before it.

There is probably less check on the rule of the simple majority in Britain than in any other democracy. There is the rule that the Queen's government must be carried on. This is a pragmatic rule to enable government to govern. It commands the assent of the minority presumably because they themselves have required the rule while in government and have every expectation of requiring it again. But even in Britain, it has been found possible to carry on government even though the largest single party did not have a majority and had to obtain such support as it could find. A requirement that legislation in Stormont had to pass by say two-thirds or three-quarters of those voting would produce a similar kind of situation.

But to place this burden on a popularly elected government requires some strong reasons in favour since, on the face of it, it makes the task of government more difficult and it is not the general rule elsewhere. It would have to be shown that it would produce the missing assent to government among the minority and that this would make the task of government easier than it is with a bare majority. It would also have to be shown that the minority were not only unlikely but unable to use the rule to frustrate the whole process of government. On a rule for a majority of those present and voting government could not be frustrated by mass abstention of opposition parties. And in the event of continued blocking there would have to be circumstances which allowed passage of legislation on appeal to Westminster.

But the intention of the requirement would be to offer the minority a part in the government of the Province. The offer of government posts to individual members of opposition parties places those members in an extremely difficult position since they do not have any parliamentary sanction with which to back their own views. But if government posts are required as a *quid pro quo* for necessary parliamentary support, then a quite different situation arises and the normal give and take of political life begins to operate. Members of government from minority parties are not separated from their parties, but must carry them if they are to remain in a coalition government and a coalition government must take their views into account.

But the requirement for a higher majority would not operate only to the benefit of the minority. If normal legislation required a two-thirds majority, then a constitutional change in the position of the province could hardly be passed by a bare majority.

At present the general assumption in Northern Ireland is that union with the Republic could be obtained by a bare majority in Stormont. Indeed, the continued return of Unionist majorities to Stormont must be in some part a reflection of that belief. The present guarantees of the British government only hold so long as a 'majority' in the Province wish to remain in the United Kingdom. In the absence of definition any majority however bare and however temporary would be enough to remove the guarantees.

The rule that the constitutional position could not be changed on a bare majority taken, as is now proposed, by referendum, would probably open up the political life of the Province. There may be many different reasons why the majority wish to remain within the UK—belief in a multi-racial community, dislike of nationalism, the higher standard of living, the special position of the Catholic Church in the Republic, ties of family and sentiment, representation in the parliament of a major power and, especially at present, a determination not to succumb to force. If, at the ballot-box, these are thought to be more important than all other election issues, then all other considerations are subsidiary to the effort to maintain the union. If, however, the Union cannot be overthrown except by, say, a two-thirds majority, then the more normal issues of politics can emerge and parliamentary seats can be won and lost on issues other than the constitutional position of the Province.

The requirement for a two-thirds—or other proportionate—majority would almost certainly reduce the power of the extreme wings and increase the power of the moderates. The coalition required for a two-thirds majority would almost certainly come from the centre. Since political power would come from accommodation and not from extreme intransigence, the political pressure towards accommodation would increase and the rewards of extremism should decline.

It would no doubt be argued that no one in the minority would undertake to support a coalition government, let alone serve in one. But the most unlikely groups have served together in coalition in the Irish Republic and indeed in the UK. If the issue of union with the Republic were to be taken out of the immediate political debate, it is most probable that there would be sufficient moderate members outside the major party who would be prepared to support and take part in a coalition government. The major issue for the minority is whether they want participation in the government of the Province in which they happen to live more than they want the chance of achieving a bare majority for union with the Republic. It is not unreasonable to suppose that a substantial number of them would take the bird in the hand in preference to a most uncertain bird in the bush. The present political upheaval started with demands for civil rights in the Province and not with demands for union with the Republic. If the minority were to refuse to take up civil rights which give them a much more powerful position than is available to any other minority in a democratic state, then the whole civil rights cause falls to the ground. It is very doubtful whether most of the minority would take this position. The requirement would not demand support from the whole minority represented at Stormont and there are strong economic reasons for remaining within the UK which must weigh with some of them once it is seen that union with Great Britain does not—as it has for the last fifty years—mean exclusion from all power in the Province.

The objection of the majority is likely to be greater and, because majorities of more than 51% are not required in other democracies for normal business, the objections are likely to be more compelling. What the majority have to decide is whether they insist on a continued monopoly of political power in the teeth of a dissident minority or a substantially reinforced assurance of union with the rest of the UK. A great many of the majority could well feel that the price for taking the disruptive issue of the border out of Northern Ireland politics was not too high. A number of other factors may influence the majority.

Although British public opinion is now far clearer on the issue in Northern Ireland and although the shooting and bombing have aroused considerable sympathy for the majority, there will be continued pressure on the British government to bring the affair to some conclusion. There is a large element of British public opinion which feels, however illogically, that 'the Irish' ought to sort out their own problems. There is also a large Irish population in Great Britain with full voting rights. All this makes it desirable for the majority to find a political solution which satisfies the minority, but preserves the union with Great Britain. It may not yet be clear to them that complete integration is unlikely to be acceptable either to British governments or to the nationalist minority. The price of union is the acquiescence of the minority and this is only likely to be given to a government in which they have some real say.

Stormont was the only Provincial government in the UK. Its original *raison d'être* has long since disappeared. Its survival has probably been due partly to the inherent difficulty of changing constitutional settlements, but also the desire of the British government to be at arms length from the Northern Ireland problem. Its utility, in the constitution of the UK, has lain in its greater ability than Westminster to produce a consensus in the Province. People in Northern Ireland would accept the decisions of their own Provincial government more readily than decisions made at Westminster. If a provincial government cannot deliver a better consensus in the province than the national government, its utility is much diminished and it is not, therefore, unreasonable for the national government to change the terms on which it functions.

The Northern Ireland government did, of course, carry out a considerable reform programme; local government elections will almost certainly give the minority for the first time control in a number of key towns. Above all, the government have been successful in restraining the majority from taking the law into their own hands despite violent provocation unknown in any other democratic community. The elections to Stor-' mont are, and always have been, by universal adult suffrage. The majority have real cause for saying that they stand for democracy against violence, for peaceful reform against violent revolution. But democracy, like justice, must not only be fair, it must be seen to be fair. There is little doubt that the half-century of parliamentary majorities have been produced by fear of exclusion from the UK rather than the merits of other policies. Within the political rules it was perfectly fair for the majority to take advantage of their opponents' inability to leave the issue alone. But after fifty years it would not be unreasonable for the Westminster government to change the rules.

Government by majority party is not an end in itself. The object of democracy is government by participation. In Northern Ireland, government by participation has been confined to one party and so, despite all that has been done, there is a case for amending the rules so that there is a greater chance for participation by those who have so far been excluded.

There may be those in the majority who would gladly make further concessions but not under violence and threat of violence. But a two-thirds or similar rule would not be a concession to violence. It would not give the extremists what they want. It would relegate the border issue. Its aim would be to disengage the moderates from the violent, those who want enlargement of civil rights by peaceable negotiation from those who want union with the Republic at whatever cost in bloodshed and disruption. This disengagement cannot come too soon if there is to be any force for moderation left among the minority or any remaining consensus between majority and minority. A solid offer of real participation in government is needed to which the non-violent minority and especially their elected leaders and their church leaders can respond. If violence ends without their help, it will be all the more difficult to rebuild the bridges between the two communities. But if violence is to end with their active assistance, it would seem that they must have a part in the provincial government in addition to the reforms at local government level.

It is difficult to see any other policy which could have the same effectiveness in producing a moderate coalition. The results of a change to proportional representation are unpredictable. It might well produce more extremists. Because the results are unpredictable it could hardly be regarded as a concession by the minority and would nonetheless be suspect by the majority. It would not produce the balancing advantage of a higher majority for constitutional change. Because of its complexity, there would be considerable delay and no effect would be felt until after a provincial general election, which would be difficult to hold at the present time. Proportional representation may be a help in the long-term but it is not an adequate answer to the short-term problem.

It may be that the present mistrust is so great that it is impossible for the minority to forgo the prospect of union with the Republic even if they have a coalition government at Stormont. It might be desirable therefore, to put a time limit of say, fifteen years on the rule requiring a higher majority. This would allow at least three general elections on the rule and give time for a coalition to prove its ability to safeguard the minority. It is most unlikely that the minority could gain even a bare majority for union with the Republic in that time, so they would have little to lose and a great deal to gain.

The time limit might not be so palatable to the majority, but it is arguable that after fifteen years of minority participation in the provincial government the border issue would die. But the issue is whether the minority want participation in provincial government sufficiently to postpone their longer-term objectives and whether the majority want assurance of continued union with Great Britain sufficiently to concede part of the provincial government to the minority.

The major long-term aims of the British government must include the withdrawal of British troops from Northern

Ireland. It is hard to see how this will happen until the citizens of Northern Ireland can take charge of their own security and it is hard to see how that can happen until there is a government in Northern Ireland which can command broad support from both communities in Northern Ireland. The Army is a very blunt instrument and it is arguable that the violence will only be brought to an ultimate end by local forces who know their way around, who have to live in the community afterwards and who have the backing of all the population.

Britain cannot afford a Palestinian-type solution just off her western coast. A quarter of a century after we pulled out, there is still fighting between Jew and Arab, which is a major hazard to international peace. But it is no longer a strategic area for us; Ireland is and always will be. So the necessity to extricate British troops is matched by a necessity to leave behind governments capable of maintaining order in the island. This cannot happen without the support of both communities and this cannot be brought about without a sharing of power in the provincial government under a constitution which makes that sharing a matter of right and not of temporary favour.

Appendix II
THE BRITISH SUBSIDIES TO NORTHERN IRELAND

Northern Ireland has an area of 3·35 million acres and a population of 1·5m. The Republic includes a region—East Leinster—similar in size (3·17m. acres) and in population (1·3 m.) to Northern Ireland and with a level of output and living standards not much lower than Northern Ireland. But the Republic also includes a hinterland four times as large as East Leinster, with a slightly larger population, and living standards 30% lower. As a result, whereas average living standards in Northern Ireland are about 20% lower than in Britain, in the Republic as a whole the 'drag' of the hinterland area brings average living standards down to about 40% below the British level.

At the same time Northern Ireland, unlike the Republic, benefits from very large subsidies from Britain. Current expenditure on its health and social services costing about £195m. in 1971/72, were subsidised to the tune of £72m. (or 37%), by Britain. In addition, the area benefited from British agricultural subsidies of over £30m.; regional employment premium assistance of £11m., and over-attribution of customs and excise revenue of about £35m. Moreover, in addition to these direct subsidies of about £150m., it made no contribution to the cost of UK defence or to certain other overheads, which in 1967/68 were estimated at £70m., and must today be much larger. The resultant figure of, perhaps, £230–240m. direct and indirect subsidies in 1971/72 may be compared with a current Northern Ireland government revenue figure of £385m. in that year.

Very large differences between the social services in Northern Ireland and the Republic are accounted for by this subsidy situation. In the Republic in 1970/71 current expenditure on health and social services cost about £205m., all of this being financed by the Republic itself. Northern Ireland, with half the population, spent £123m. of its own—viz. about the same percentage of its gross domestic product as the Republic—plus £72m. derived from the British government. Thus *per capita* its health and social welfare expenditure was almost double the Republic's figure.

For the Republic to undertake the subsidisation of Northern Ireland on the same scale as at present would impose a very heavy burden indeed. In 1971/72 current government expenditure in the Republic totalled £570m., so that the provision of the £150m. direct subsidies from the UK would have increased current expenditure in the Republic by 26½%. Even allowing for the fact that the share of the overhead of expenditure on defence attributable to Northern Ireland might be much lower if it were associated with the Republic than is the case now that it is in the UK, it is clear that even on the most favourable assumptions the Republic would have to incur some additional expenditure on defence, etc., in the event of reunification, which would bring this figure of additional expenditure up above 30%.

This 30% increase in current government expenditure would merely suffice to keep Northern Ireland in the condition to which it has been accustomed. If at the same time the Republic were to seek to raise its *own* standards of health and social service expenditure to the level it would be financing in Northern Ireland this would add a further £145m. or 25%. This figure makes no allowance for the achievement of parity with Northern Ireland in respect of such matters as housing or educational services. The maintenance of Northern Ireland health and social services at parity with Britain, and the achievement of similar parity for the Republic would thus, if it were to be financed solely by the Republic, cost it an additional £300 m. odd, increasing the Republic's present tax burden by well over 50%.

It is this situation that makes it necessary to contemplate a prolonged period of external assistance for the provision of health and social services in Northern Ireland in the event of reunification. This would have to continue for something like a quarter of a century even on the basis of an Irish growth rate about 40% greater than that of Great Britain—the ratio between the two island's growth rates that was actually achieved during most of the 1960s.

Appendix III
ECONOMIC IMPLICATIONS OF THE CONFLICT

The conflict in Northern Ireland has had a disastrous effect on the province's economic development. In June 1971, a commission was appointed by the government of Northern Ireland to review the prospects for economic and social development in the area. This commission reported in December 1971 (Government of Northern Ireland White Paper, Cmd. 564) and one of its first conclusions was that '... the flow of new industrial investment from outside Northern Ireland had practically dried up and that in the conditions created by civil unrest there was little likelihood of any revival for some time after peace was restored to the streets'.

Of the *private sector* the commission stated that '... there is a grave danger that the momentum generated during the 1960s has now been lost ...'. Of the *public sector*, it declared that '... private industrial and commercial investment is drying up and recovery will be slow'. A short-term recommendation made by the commission was the creation of a Northern Ireland Finance Corporation which would offer financial assistance to undertakings threatened with closure or contraction. Some £50 million was to have been earmarked for its use.

There are three main problem areas:

(i) Labour
October 1971 the number of unemployed in Northern Ireland had risen to 43,000, or 8·7% of the working population—the highest level since 1940. To that figure may be added the large number of women who are unemployed but who have not registered and the 3,000 school leavers who came on to the labour market in September 1971. The percentage of unemployed is considerably higher in some of the poorer urban areas, notably in the Bogside and the Creggan districts of Londonderry.

(ii) Investment

In a period of eighteen months (January 1970–June 1971) the Belfast Chamber of Commerce stated that no new external investment had been made in Northern Ireland. Over the decade in the 1960s, external investment reached £200m. of which £120m. came from the United States. The Northern Ireland Minister of Commerce said that there had been a complete 'loss of confidence' in the area. Against this the City of Londonderry appears as an anomaly; although 13·8% of the working population is unemployed, investment in the area is high. Du Pont recently brought their investment in synthetic rubber and fibre up to £27m. and claimed to have created 1,600 jobs. Elsewhere in Northern Ireland, from 1969–71, 1,200 jobs were lost after companies cancelled expansion plans or decided not to go ahead with new projects. In compensating businesses and private individuals, the British government is believed to have paid out some £50m.

(iii) Bankruptcies

Although no complete figures were available, the financial year 1970–71 is considered to have been one of the worst periods for bankruptcies in Ulster's history. Most of the firms affected were small family businesses with little reserve liquidity. Over 200 public houses have been damaged in street warfare, and many of these have not reopened. One of the most serious consequences of the conflict has been the decline in retail trade.

The Belfast Bus Corporation has had 38 vehicles damaged. The replacement cost was £500,000 and the Corporation claimed to have lost revenue amounting to £1·5m. Another serious drain on public revenue was the rent strike begun in August 1971, by some 22,000 Catholic households. By April 1972 this was estimated to have cost the Belfast Corporation over £1m.

In an effort to encourage investment and industrial expansion the Northern Ireland Ministry of Commerce launched, in April 1972, a press publicity campaign describing some of the areas in which progress had been made in spite of the conflict; manufacturing output rose by 7·2% in 1970 and by

6·1% in 1971; industrial productivity was said to be up by 6·7% in 1972; and in the same year, some 7,000 new jobs were said to have been created in manufacturing by expanding existing plant. But those figures could not camouflage the absence of new investment.

Appendix IV
ESSENTIAL DATA

1. People and Government

The island of Ireland (Eire) has a total area of 32,595 sq. miles, divided into 32 counties, with a total population of approximately 4·5 million. Four historic provinces are recognised, although their boundaries have now no administrative significance: Connacht in the west (five counties), Munster in the south (six), Leinster in the east (twelve) and Ulster in the north (nine).

For half a century six of Ulster's nine counties have been politically detached as an integral part of the United Kingdom with a measure of domestic autonomy. Area: 5,459 sq. miles. Population (census 9 October 1966): 1,484,775.

The remaining 26 counties constitute an independent sovereign republic. Area: 27,136 sq. miles. Population (census 17 April 1966): 2,884,002.

Northern Ireland.—Until the end of the sixteenth century, Ulster was the centre of the most intransigent resistance to English rule. There was no sharp ethnic or linguistic distinction between the people of Ulster on the one hand and of south-west Scotland, the Highlands and the Hebrides on the other. Radical change was brought by the Reformation in Britain, the defeat in 1603 of the anti-English rebellion led by the chiefs of O'Neill and O'Donnell, and the regnal union in 1605 of England and Scotland. In 1608 there began the plantation of Ulster with Protestant settlers from the Scottish Lowlands and England, expelling the native Catholic and Gaelic-speaking people to the poorer lands of the south and west.

The old Gaelic order of Ireland had been crushed. Ulster became in effect a British province. But the enforcement of the Penal Laws throughout the eighteenth century, together with the influence of Enlightenment ideas spreading from America and France, on occasion led Ulster Dissenters to make common cause with Catholics: the rebellion of the republican United Irishmen in 1798, for example, was led by middle-class Ulster Presbyterians inspired by the French Revolution.

Catholic emancipation and the growth of militant Irish

nationalism saw religion restored in the latter half of the nineteenth century, as the dominant (and divisive) factor in Ulster affairs. In the 1850s a pattern of sectarian rioting was established which has persisted to the present day. In 1885 religious and political divisions were clearly identified when Lord Randolph Churchill elected to 'play the Orange card' against Gladstone's proposals for Irish Home Rule—that is, to rouse the lodges of the Protestant Orange Order against the government, and also against the predominantly Catholic nationalists in Ulster. In 1914, with the passage of the third Home Rule Bill, the Orange-Unionist Protestant Ascendancy of Ulster, with the active support of many leading members of the Conservative opposition at Westminster, threatened armed rebellion. The operation of the Act was suspended.

After the First World War, however, following the overwhelming victory of the nationalist Sinn Féin party in 1918 and the subsequent guerrilla war against the British power, the Ulster Unionists in 1920 reluctantly accepted the provisions of the Government of Ireland Act. Under this measure, which superseded the Home Rule Act of 1914, Ireland was to have two parliaments subordinate to Westminster—one in Belfast for six of Ulster's nine counties, and one in Dublin for the remaining 26 counties of Ireland.

In the six Ulster counties the 1921 elections resulted in a Unionist majority of 40 to 12 over Sinn Féin, and the government of Northern Ireland, now a federal province of the UK, came into being against a background of civil war and sectarian disorder.

Under the 1920 Act, legislative power is divided between the UK parliament at Westminster and the subordinate parliament at Stormont in Belfast. Executive power is vested in a Governor, on behalf of the Queen, advised by nine ministers responsible to parliament. The Stormont parliament consists of two houses: the House of Commons, with 52 members, elected by universal suffrage for a term not exceeding five years; and the Senate, consisting of two *ex officio* members and 24 elected by the House of Commons by the proportional representation system. Northern Ireland sends 12 elected members to the House of Commons at Westminster.

Since the creation of the Stormont legislature the government of Northern Ireland has been, by a succession of large majorities, in the hands of the Ulster Unionist Party. Its autonomous authority is limited to the purely domestic affairs of the province; matters touching the Crown, external trade, defence, the armed forces, etc., being reserved to the UK parliament at Westminster. Taxation is imposed and collected by the UK government, which in turn finances the Northern Ireland public and social services.

Irish Republic.—In the 1921 elections Sinn Féin won an overwhelming victory in the 26 counties, capturing all but four seats, confirming its rejection of the Government of Ireland Act, and continuing the armed struggle against the British power. A truce was arranged in July, and prolonged negotiations ended in December with the Irish plenipotentiaries' acceptance of Lloyd George's offer of 'Dominion status' similar to that of Canada.

Eamon de Valera, president of Dáil Éireann, the revolutionary legislature, opposed the Treaty, but the Dáil approved it by 64 votes to 57. Sinn Féin thereupon split into a pro-Treaty party and a republican party, the former constituting the provisional government. Civil war broke out in June 1922, but four months later the leader of the pro-Treaty party (and head of the provisional government) was able to summon Dáil Éireann and ratify the constitution of the Irish Free State (Saorstat Éireann). The republicans continued the civil war for some time against the Free State government power, and for longer still against the Unionist authority in Northern Ireland.

The Anglo-Irish Treaty of 1921 was followed in October 1922 by the enactment by Dáil Éireann of a constitution establishing the Irish Free State (Saorstat Éireann). This provided for the representation of the monarch by a governor-general and required all members of the legislature to take an oath of allegiance to the Crown. The civil war between the pro-Treaty wing of Sinn Féin (which now formed the government of the Irish Free State under William T. Cosgrave) and the republican wing (led by Eamon de Valera) ended in 1923 with the submission of the republicans, who continued, however, to boycott the Dáil.

It was hoped by the Free State government that the Boundary Commission of 1924–25 would transfer to its authority those areas of Northern Ireland which were predominantly Catholic and Nationalist—i.e. Derry City, Co. Tyrone and Co. Fermanagh, South Down and South Armagh. This, it was thought, would induce Stormont to seek a federal compromise with Dublin and enter an all-Ireland parliament. No report, however, was published by the Commission, and in December 1925 the Free State government formally recognised the Border as delineated by the 1920 Government of Ireland Act.

In 1927 de Valera broke with the intransigent republicans and led his party, under the name of Fianna Fáil, back into the Dáil in opposition to the pro-Treaty party (which assumed the name first of Cumann na nGael and then of Fine Gael, by which it is still known). Since then Fianna Fáil and Fine Gael have been the dominating parties, divided less by any doctrinal differences than by rancours persisting from the Treaty quarrel, the breaking of the original Sinn Féin movement and the civil war that followed. They are both essentially centre parties, Fianna Fáil now tending to the right, Fine Gael to the left. The republican intransigents, many of whom adhered to James Connolly's syndicalist dream of an all-Ireland workers' republic, remained under the banner of Sinn Féin, its underground militant wing appropriating the name of the Irish Republican Army.

In 1932 de Valera's Fianna Fáil came to power with an overall majority, and, with the exception of two spells of opposition (1948–51 and 1954–57) to inter-party administrations headed by Fine Gael, it has been the governing party ever since. The keystone of de Valera's policy was unchanged: the creation of a republic in 'external association' with the British Commonwealth and the peaceful reunification of Ireland.

The Fianna Fáil government assumed the right to repudiate the limitations laid down by the 1921 Treaty. The oath of allegiance was abolished together with the right of appeal to the judicial committee of the Privy Council; Irish nationality was distinguished from British; and the office of governor-general was abolished. In 1937 a new constitution declaring Ireland to be 'a sovereign, independent, democratic state' was adopted by plebiscite; and in 1949 Ireland was declared a republic (a step regarded by Britain as placing it outside the Commonwealth).

2. Political Movements

Sinn Féin (Gaelic: 'Ourselves') took over the effective leadership of the Irish nationalist movement from the Irish Parliamentary Party after the death of Parnell. Its founder Arthur Griffith was a militant nationalist but not a republican. He aimed at something like the old Austro-Hungarian dual monarchy. The first open split in the movement came when the republican wing led by Eamon de Valera refused to accept the Anglo-Irish Treaty of 1921 and precipitated the civil war of 1922–23. The name of Sinn Féin was then largely appropriated by the republicans. Following the return of de Valera and the majority of his followers to parliamentary politics and constitutionalism, the label of Sinn Féin was taken over by the dissident rump of intransigents. Since then the leadership of Sinn Féin has steadily moved to the left and is now dominated by Communists.

The Irish Republican Army is the name of the illegal military instrument of Sinn Féin. Following a split in the movement at the end of 1969 the IRA organisation in Belfast is largely in the hands of the 'Provisionals' who are traditionalists and oppose the 'Officials' or 'Regulars' with their Marxist policy of 'national liberation'. Current intelligence estimates of the numbers of IRA men active in Ulster around 1,000 Provisionals and 500 Officials, as well as the 'migration force' operating from the Republic. Many of these can be identified on sight.

The official wing of the IRA has been dominated by Marxists since 1963 and aims to create a 'united socialist Ireland' in which the Southern Catholic working class would co-exist with the Protestant working class in the North. The officials are known to co-operate with the Communists to achieve their ends; they advocate the nationalisation of all resources, the confiscation of private property, and disengagement from power *blocs*. They are opposed to Irish entry into the EEC. *Cathal Goulding* has been Chief of Staff of the IRA since 1966. Goulding is a Marxist-Leninist and has been a member of the IRA for over thirty years.

The *Provisional* wing of the IRA appeared in December 1969 and is a more traditional, nationalist, Irish movement with considerable support in the rural areas. The declared Provisional aim is a democratic socialist Republic. Since the split in the IRA, the Provisionals have become the more violent faction, responsible for the greater proportion of the bombings, shootings and bank raids in Ulster. The Provisional political platform has been rudimentary and the attempts to formulate one have caused dissension within the movement. The Provisionals have four principal leaders: *Rory Brady (Ruari O Bradaigh)*, born in 1932, used to be a technical school teacher. He is the President of the Provisional Sinn Féin (the Provisional political wing). He twice served as IRA Chief of Staff before the split in 1969. *Joe Cahill*, born in 1920, was formerly a construction foreman and has been a leading militant of the IRA for over thirty years. In 1942, Cahill was captured and sentenced to death following a gun battle in which a policeman was killed, but he was reprieved. Cahill has given warning that the Provisional IRA would extend guerrilla warfare to Britain if necessary. Formerly the Provisional commander in Belfast, Cahill now lives in Dublin. *John Stephenson (Sean MacStiofain)* is in his early forties and is believed to be the moving force behind Provisional strategy. MacStiofain is Catholic and anti-Communist. *David O'Connell (Daithi O'Conaill)* is treasurer of the Provisionals and a teacher of building and construction. He was wounded in the 1956 IRA campaign and in 1960 was sentenced to eight years' imprisonment for possessing arms and explosives (he served only three years). In October 1971, O'Connell was involved in the Czech arms deal uncovered at Schiphol Airport, Amsterdam.

Much of the IRA finance has traditionally come from overseas, mainly from the USA. Since the split in the IRA, most Irish-American aid has gone to the Provisionals. There are two principal societies of sympathisers in the USA; the *Irish Republican Aid Committee (IRAC)*, which favours the Officials, and the *Irish Northern Aid Committee (INAC)*, which was founded in 1969 and which supports the Provisionals. Within Ulster and the Republic some money is raised by donations but much of it comes from protection rackets, intimidation and theft. In the period from March 1970–Autumn 1971, the Provisionals claimed to have received £150,000–£200,000 as a result of bank and post office robberies.

Fianna Fáil, the ruling party in the Irish Republic, descends from the republican wing of the old Sinn Féin movement. Its founder and for many years its leader, Eamon de Valera, is now President of the Republic. Under de Valera and his successors Seán Lemass and Jack Lynch (now Prime Minister of the Republic), Fianna Fáil has maintained a pragmatic, liberal-conservative attitude, and is now largely identified with business interests in the Republic.

Fine Gael, the main opposition party in the Republic, descends from Arthur Griffith's pro-Treaty wing of the old Sinn Féin movement. It formed the government during the early years of the Irish Free State, but since 1932, when it first lost to Fianna Fáil, it has seldom been in power. Like Fianna Fáil, it is essentially a party of the centre. Its leader, Liam Cosgrave, is the son of William T. Cosgrave, the first head of government in the Irish Free State.

The Labour Party has a weak representation in Dáil Éireann. It lost ground at the 1969 general election following its adoption of an explicitly Socialist ideology. Most observers are sceptical about its chances in future elections, but some of its more ambitious members are hopeful of being able to form a government coalition with Fine Gael if the present crisis results in Jack Lynch's fall and in Fianna Fáil's losing ground at an early election.

The Civil Rights movement in Northern Ireland was virtually taken over by Communist and leftist elements following the first outbreaks of communal disorder in 1968. This was also largely true of the Citizens' Defence Committees, formed to organise the defence of Catholic communities against Protestant extremists. For a time it seemed as if they would continue as instruments of the Communist-dominated 'popular front' of Sinn Féin and such revolutionary leftist groups in the north as People's Democracy with which Miss Bernadette Devlin is closely identified. But more recently an anti-Communist counter-attack, in which the agents of Fianna Fáil seem to have been heavily involved, has strengthened the leadership of moderate Catholic Nationalists.

The *Northern Ireland Civil Rights Association* (*NICRA*) emerged in 1967 as a mainly Catholic, middle-class movement which included Unionists and Republicans and which campaigned on a broad platform for the maintenance of civil liberties. By 1972 the 14-member NICRA executive contained at least eight members of the Official IRA and two known Communists. The principal members of the NICRA Central Executive are: *Kevin Boyle* of the People's Democracy. Boyle was born in 1943; he is a lecturer in law at Queen's University, Belfast, and has links with the International Marxists Group. *Ann Hope* is treasurer of NICRA and a Communist sympathiser and is believed to have connections with the Official IRA. *Edwina Stewart* is secretary of the NICRA and was vice-chairman of the Northern Ireland Communist Party.

The *Northern Resistance Movement* (*NRM*) emerged in 1970 as a splinter of NICRA following disagreement over the extent to which NICRA should involve itself in Southern politics. By October 1971, the NRM had become dominated by the People's Democracy which had allied itself with the Provisionals, to form the *Northern Resistance Committee* (*NRC*).

The *Nationalist Party* of Northern Ireland descends from the old Irish Parliamentary Party and seeks reunification of Ireland by peaceful constitutional means. During the troubles of 1969 it lost ground somewhat to leftist extremists, but more recently has rallied support among Catholic moderates.

Revolutionary republican organisations such as the *Connolly Association* and *Wolf Tone League* tended formerly to be syndicalist or Trotskyist in character, but during the past three years they have been deeply infiltrated, like Sinn Féin, by the Communist apparatus.

The *Unionist Party*, which has provided the government of Northern Ireland since the creation of the semi-autonomous legislature half a century ago, is linked to the *Orange Order*, a society dedicated to the defence of the constitution and the preservation of the Protestant ascendancy in the province. During the long leadership of Lord Brookeborough its face was turned firmly against such social and political reforms as would strengthen the voice of the large Catholic (and for the most part also Nationalist) minority. Under Captain Terence O'Neill, who initiated a series of conversations with prime ministers of the Republic, however, it assumed a more liberal complexion. Captain O'Neill's mild reformist policy precipitated a crisis within the party which was exacerbated by the breakdown of law and order in large areas of Londonderry and Belfast last year. When his position became all but untenable he resigned, but his policies have been continued by Major James Chichester-Clark (now Lord Moyola), the former Prime Minister of Northern Ireland, and his successor, Mr Brian Faulkner.

Paisleyites is the name by which members of the intransigent *Protestant Unionist Party* are commonly known. (It is also commonly if inaccurately applied as a derogatory term to the hard-line members of the Unionist Party's local associations, whose opposition to reforms in the political interests of the Catholic community is most powerfully voiced by William Craig, a former government minister dismissed by Captain O'Neill and more recently expelled from the Unionist Parliamentary Party). The Protestant Unionists are led by the Rev. Ian Paisley, moderator of the Free Presbyterian Church of Northern Ireland, and one of Northern Ireland's most powerful and effective politicians. Mr Paisley sits in the Stormont legislature for Captain Terence (now Lord) O'Neill's former constituency of Bannside. In the UK general election of June 1970 he defeated the Unionist candidate (and also the Northern Ireland Labour, National Democrat and Liberal candidates) in the constituency of North Antrim. Mr Paisley's victory and Miss Bernadette Devlin's increased majority in Mid-Ulster have been widely taken as omens of coming conflict.

Behind the most militant Protestants stands the clandestine well-armed *Ulster Volunteer Force*, opposed equally to Catholic

Nationalists and the Communist-leftist coalition of Sinn Féin and other revolutionary groups in the north. It now appears to have been superseded by Mr William Craig's *Vanguard Movement* which organised a two-day work stoppage in association with Mr Billy Hull's Union of Loyalist Workers after the imposition of direct rule. Then there are equally shadowy groups such as the *Ulster Protestant Volunteers* and the *Shankhill Defence Association*. Mr John McKeague, the leader of the Shankhill Defence Association, publishes a paper with a circulation of about 6,000 and has declared that his organisation would take the offensive in the event of 'a complete breakdown of law and order'. The '*Tartan Gangs*' of Protestant youths have also become more militant. It is very hard to estimate the strength of any of these groups.

Appendix V
AN ULSTER CHRONOLOGY

1931 The IRA was declared illegal in Eire.

1949 Ireland Act said *inter alia:*
  (1) The border could not be changed without the consent of Stormont.
  (2) The UK would not intervene in Northern Ireland internal affairs except to control a breakdown of law and order.

1951 Public Order Act forbade wearing uniforms showing connection with political organisations or object. Notice required of all processions.

1954–58 The IRA started raids in Ulster. 187 people were interned in Ulster and 206 in Eire.

1963 Captain O'Neill became Premier of Northern Ireland.
  Beginnings of Civil Rights movement.

1965 Captain O'Neill invited Sean Lemass, Prime Minister of Eire to go to Belfast to discuss matters of common interest. The question of the border was not on the agenda.

1966 The Rev. Ian Paisley organised demonstrations against 'Romeward' trend in the Presbyterian Church. Convicted of unlawful assembly and later imprisoned. Captain O'Neill proscribed extremist Ulster Volunteer Force.

1967 Formation of Northern Ireland Civil Rights Movement.

1968 Civil Rights March in Londonderry, in October, although banned by Mr Craig, Minister of Home Affairs. The Royal Ulster Constabulary (RUC) reacted roughly and there were more demonstrations in Belfast.

  In November the Londonderry Commission was set up to deal with economic grievances. An Ombudsman was appointed to investigate grievances. Mr Paisley led a march against the reforms. Mr Craig was dismissed and Captain O'Neill embarked

1968	on a programme of reforms dealing with housing and local government. These were not enough for the Civil Rights movement.
1969	A Civil Rights march from Belfast to Londonderry was permitted in January. There was a clash at Burntollet between the marchers and Protestant Ultras. The RUC entered the Bogside where a later Commission of Enquiry alleged that assaults and misconduct occurred.
Apr.	Captain O'Neill resigned and was replaced by Major Chichester-Clarke. Miss Bernadette Devlin secured a seat at Westminster.
Aug.	The annual march of the Apprentice Boys of Derry was scheduled to take place. There were fights in the Bogside between Catholics and the RUC. Nobody was killed but much material damage was done.
	Subsequently the RUC and Catholics fought it out in Belfast in the Falls and Shanklin Roads. Seven people were killed. The popularity of the Provisional IRA dates from this event. CS gas was used for the first time.
	British troops were sent in to keep the peace sharing responsibility for security with Stormont. (Constitutionally Stormont was responsible for security.) The Army was welcomed by the Catholics at this time.
	The Cameron Commission was set up to investigate the disorders.
Sept.	Further riots in Londonderry.
Oct.	The B Specials were disbanded. Measures were taken to recruit a new force, known as the Ulster Defence Regiment.
	From 1969 it was alleged that the IRA worked to infiltrate the Civil Rights Movements and the Citizens' Defence Committees.
Nov.	RUC disarmed.
1970	
Jan.	Tomas MacGiolla, President of Sinn Féin, ad-

1970   dressed the annual conference in Marxist terms, thereby antagonising those of his followers who regarded the abolition of the border as the overriding objective. The Provisional IRA effectively assumed leadership of the Northern Catholics.

Various acts were passed during this period to restrain riots and discourage dissension.

1969 Firearms Act.

1970 Prevention of Incitement to Hatred Act.

Apr.   The truce between the British Army and the Catholics was broken by riots at Ballymurphy estate in Belfast. The Rev. Ian Paisley was elected to Westminster.

General Freeland, commanding the British Army in Belfast, said Northern Ireland must solve its own problems. The Army could not stay there for ever. This remark caused much gloom.

May   Mr Lynch dismissed Mr Haughey and Mr Blaney from his cabinet on charges of complicity in gun-running to the North. Mr Boland resigned in sympathy. The government of Eire considered the possibility of internment.

June   Minimum Sentences Act, enjoining mandatory sentences for rioters. Mr Frank McManus, Civil Rights leader, elected to Westminster. Riots in Belfast. Five people were killed and 248 injured. On 27 June, mobs moved to an orgy of destruction. In Ballymacarett, soldiers were fired on by snipers using machine guns. CS gas was used to disperse crowds.

July   The Army searched Lower Falls for arms. The Catholics replied by stoning. The riots assume a different character.

They were more organised, more directed against the troops.

IRA snipers appeared in neighbouring buildings and there was systematic arson.

Aug.   Ban on marches was defied by Protestants in Londonderry.

1970   Mr. Roy Porter resigned as Minister for Home Affairs for health reasons.

The Black Watch were accused of looting.

23 Aug.   A ban on all parades and marches for six months was imposed by Stormont.

Oct.   The IRA moved to selective terrorism.

Dec.   Stormont introduced major reforms for local government.

Mr Lynch spoke of possibility of internment in the South for the IRA.

Minimum Sentences Act was amended. Mandatory sentences only for riotous behaviour.

1971   There was the first big Protestant riot for 5 months
Jan.   in Ballymurphy, Belfast.

In the first ten weeks 21 people were killed in political violence, most of whom were Protestants.

6 Feb.   First British soldier shot.

25 Feb.   Housing Executive Act. All public house building and allocation to be the responsibility of one central housing organisation.

23 Feb.   Mr Lynch spoke of amending the constitution of the Irish Republic to suit Northerners, e.g. the position of the Roman Catholic Church. He referred to a 'new kind of Irish society equally agreeable to North and South'. Mr Lynch had problems in his own party over divorce reform and contraception. The Army said that tension in the Catholic areas of Belfast was as high as when the troops arrived, with the Provisional wing of the IRA now the acknowledged opponent. It was behind the stone-throwing of the children. It bombarded the troops with petrol-bombs, nail-bombs, gelignite and gun-fire. The blowing up of customs-posts became frequent.

Under a use of the Special Powers Act, it became illegal to conceal dead or wounded persons. Funeral processions were to be curbed as they were a fruitful source of riot. Also the wearing of para-military uniforms. The last was hard to enforce.

1971   The head of the Irish Special Branch accused Mr
        Haughey of offering £50,000 to help the IRA. Mr
        Lynch told the Provisionals that they had no back-
        ing for violence.

        The Provisionals claimed to control the Ardoyne,
        Ballymurphy and the New Lodge areas of Belfast
        while the Officials controlled the Falls Road area.

        General Tuzo replaced General Crum as GOC
        because of the illness of the latter, almost as soon
        as he took office.

        The government refused to round up licensed guns,
        despite the ire of opposition MPs who feared that
        some of the clubs were fronts for illegal, para-mili-
        tary organisations.

Mar.   Major Chichester-Clarke announced a three-point
        drive against the IRA, including the permanent
        presence of troops in the no-go areas.

        A big trade fair was announced to encourage
        flagging trade.

8 Mar. 5,000 Orange Marchers set out on a parade.
        Earlier there was a protest march by women
        wearing IRA uniform in defiance of the ban.
        More troops were sent out during this period.

10 Mar. The feud between the Officials and the Provisionals
        broke out into open violence. There were murder-
        ous street battles in which it was estimated that
        40 to 50 members lost their lives.

11 Mar. Three young soldiers were ambushed and mur-
        dered. Mr Maudling acted to remove soldiers
        under 18 from service in Ulster.

        There was a grandiose funeral of an IRA man.
        4,500 troops stood by.

13 Mar. Over 6,000 shipyard workers, Protestant and
        Catholic marched through the streets of Belfast
        to demand the internment of the IRA.

16 Mar. A reward of £50,000 was offered by Stormont for
        information about terrorists.

        Major Chichester-Clarke was attacked by his
        own party, particularly by Mr John Taylor for

1971	being too soft. The existence of the no-go areas was the main charge against him.
20 Mar.	Mr Maudling flew out to Ulster in an attempt to save the Premier.
22 Mar.	Major Chichester-Clarke resigned and was replaced by Mr Faulkner, defeating Mr Craig. He included in his cabinet Mr Bleakley, not a Unionist, to be Minister of Community Relations, and also Mr West, a right-winger, as Minister of Agriculture.
31 Mar.	Mr Faulkner announced a 7-day amnesty.
Apr.	Mr Maudling announced that there were no areas of no-go.
10 Apr.	There were fears of marches in memory of the 1916 Easter Rising. The police called for limited arms. About 18,000 troops were on red alert and stepped up searches for arms and explosives. There was a secret meeting of the two IRA factions. It was alleged that the three young soldiers were killed in retaliation for IRA men shot during riots.
22 Apr.	The Irish government offered to pay for a British launch wrecked by IRA saboteurs. The illegal possession of arms was to be punished more severely in Eire.
8 May	Mr Craig failed to secure election to the party executive committee. The RUC had still not recovered from its reorganisation. It was about 3,000 strong and was still not yet on the beat in the no-go areas. It was on patrol in the Bogside for the first time since 1958. The newly raised Ulster Defence Regiment was recruiting well at this time and was expected to have about 5,000 men by the end of the year. Its main task was to guard vulnerable points and road-blocks.
21 May	16 people were arrested in the worst disturbances since Easter.
24 May	Allegations of brutality were made against the Royal Highland Fusiliers. The Republicans called for UN observers in Ulster.

1971	
31 May	Police in mining areas were investigating reports that gelignite was being stolen from mines in England and sold to IRA sympathisers.
2 June	600 Green Jackets arrived to replace the second battalion, Parachute Regiment. There was a clash between Orangemen and the troops at the Catholic town of Dungiven, at an illegal Orange parade.
	Cardinal Conway said that it might be worth trying to have mixed schools.
	Many discoveries of arms caches were made in this period.
23 June	Mr Faulkner said that he wanted to win over Catholics. Opposition MPs would have a bigger say in running the province through a new system of parliamentary committees dealing with social, environmental, and industrial services. He offered them chairmanships.
14 July	The Social and Democratic Labour Party said it would withdraw from Stormont over the shooting at Derry of civilians. An official enquiry was refused.
16 July	IRA men posing as doctors removed from a Belfast hospital one of their number.
23 July	In a series of raids on selected houses the Northern Ireland security forces found IRA documents and radio equipment. Water-cannon and rubber bullets were now being used in crowd control.
24 July	A massive round-up of suspects was begun.
26 July	According to the captured documents the IRA planned to launch a terror campaign in England. They might also have been robbing banks for funds.
	More was heard of internment. Mr Maudling said that if it were necessary no advance warning would be given.
	The Army reported that an attempt had been made to ambush one of its patrols near the border with the Irish Republic.
9 Aug.	All-day battles in Belfast and Derry marked the

1971	bloodiest day yet with 10 killed. Internment was introduced. 300 arrests were made but 70 were released in a couple of days. The IRA had running battles with the Army in the streets.
9–18 Aug.	Many refugees were fleeing to Eire, the Irish government setting up camps for them. (Most later returned.)

The Officials denounced the plans of sabotage in the UK.

In Derry some areas were still under IRA control with IRA manned checkpoints at the border areas. Strikes in these areas were encouraged by the IRA. Mr Faulkner had angry exchanges with Mr Lynch who denounced internment and called for the abolition of Stormont. Mr Heath accused Mr Lynch of interfering with British affairs. The Army Chief said that the IRA was virtually beaten. But the leader of the Provisionals was at this time holding his own conference with newspapermen.

18 Aug.	Mr Fitt withdrew from the government in protest at the shootings at Derry.

Mr Faulkner issued a White Paper setting out in detail the progress which had been made. Mr Heath refused to recall parliament to discuss Northern Ireland. The Labour opposition accused the government of being partisan on the Unionist side.

There were at least 30 deaths in riots after the introduction of internment.

In London it was announced that an inquiry under Sir Edmund Compton would be held into allegations of brutality in the internment process.

Mr Lynch supported the campaign of civil disobedience. This campaign included the nonpayment of rates and rents. Local government was dislocated by the withdrawal of non-Unionist Councillors so that no quorum could be convened which meant that essential payments could not be

1971   authorised. This campaign particularly angered the Protestants.

The internees staged hunger strikes. The IRA were sniping at lone soldiers instead of attacking patrols. Eire was said to be sacking soldiers with IRA sympathies.

It was reported that Catholics were still joining the Ulster Defence Regiment which was under the command of Brigadier Ormerod, a Catholic.

26 Aug.   Mr Craig said that the Ulster Defence Regiment was a political blind and that he might have to recommend people to withdraw from it.

An Act was passed whereby compensation was to be given for malicious damage to private property. A soldier, Colonel Vincent, speaking of Anderstown, a suburb of Belfast, in January 1971 said that recruiting by the IRA was at its most intense from April to late July.

The ratio of people who were recruited prior to internment in August and afterwards was probably more than ten to one.

1 Sept.   An appeal to the High Court in London that the internment measures were illegal was dismissed.

Mr Lynch accused British troops of 30 border incursions. It was suggested that UN troops should police borders. Mr Heath and Mr Lynch agreed to meet on 6 Sept. for two days.

8 Sept.   The IRA made threats against civilian clerks working with the Army in Ulster.

There were further serious explosions in the centre of Belfast and random terrorist shootings.

Mr Joe Cahill, leader of the Provisionals, was ordered out of the USA. Irish Americans were reported cold to Mr Cahill and Miss Devlin because they referred to the police as pigs.

The 100th death in civil strife was reported from Ulster.

The two Prime Ministers agreed to meet with Mr Faulkner at the end of the month.

1971

13 Sept.   Cardinal Conway condemned the violence.

14 Sept.   Mr John Taylor urged the blowing up of border tracks and the establishment of a third force.

15 Sept.   The Joint Security Council asked the Ulster gun clubs voluntarily to suspend their activities. Mr Fitt condemned the Provisionals and backed the Cardinal's statement.

16 Sept.   The IRA kidnapped a PC and took him across the Ulster border.

The number of internees was stated to be 220. Mr Faulkner was considering cuts in benefit to defeat the Ulster rent strikers.

Lord Denning ruled that English courts had no power to order the release of two Irishmen arrested and detained in Northern Ireland as 'suspects' by British soldiers. The use of CS gas was cleared for open-air crowd control.

17 Sept.   The Opposition MPs and Senators formed an alternative Parliament called 'The Assembly of Northern Irish people'.

It was estimated that 8,000 people had fled from the centre of Belfast in the last six weeks. The lines between the Protestant and Catholic working-classes were now rigidly drawn.

There were more attacks on customs-buildings. One, at Belleek, used 150 pounds of explosive, about twice the size of anything recorded previously.

21 Sept.   The Army accused the IRA of using dum-dum bullets, but they denied this.

23 Sept.   Mr Maudling said that the British government was prepared to discuss constitutional changes so that the Catholic minority should have an active, permanent place in the public affairs of Ulster. The problem was to broaden the base of government without alienating the right-wing Protestant elements.

24 Sept.   Mr Heath wound up the emergency debate on Ulster. Internment had only been introduced reluctantly at the request of the Northern Ireland government.

1971 27 Sept.	Mr David Bleakley resigned from the government six weeks after internment.
	Mr Lynch said that the refusal of the opposition to join in discussions was an obstacle to progress. Mr Fitt denied this.
	The Army was disturbed by an opinion poll which said that the majority of British people wanted the Army to leave, though few criticised its behaviour.
29 Sept.	Tripartite talks began at Chequers and there was an amicable discussion on ending terrorism. Mr Lynch promised to look into the question of explosives control. It was believed that Mr Lynch brought up the question of UN observers in Ulster. Mr Maudling spoke of talking to minority groups about their possible role in the public life of Northern Ireland.
	The IRA used a bazooka in Belfast. The Army noted the sophistication of weapons used.
30 Sept.	A jury failed to bring in a verdict in Belfast in the first prosecution under the Prevention of Incitement to Hatred Act. The accused were granted bail pending a new trial.
2 Oct.	A paratrooper gave his life in an effort to save some children.
6 Oct.	Tripartite talks with Mr Lynch, Mr Faulkner and Mr Heath.
	Mr Faulkner said that the Army would step-up its war with the IRA and hinted that the vigilante system might be legalised as an intelligence organisation. The Dublin government expressed alarm.
7 Oct.	It was announced in Parliament that 3 more battalions would be sent to Ulster, bringing the strength up to 13,600.
8 Oct.	Security coverage was sought for police stations, badly battered by recent attacks.
10 Oct.	The Army found a new type of bomb, more dangerous to the planter than to the dismantler, called the Castlerobin.
12 Oct.	Mr Roy Bradford, the Ulster Minister of Develop-

1971	ment said that the country was on the brink of economic bankruptcy. Westminster should give more support to Stormont.
13 Oct.	Mr Craig attacked Mr Faulkner in a vote of censure that failed.

11 out of 12 Opposition MPs stayed away from Stormont.

The Army bomb disposal unit team protested that explosives could not be traced back to their last legal owners and ICI therefore withdrew all stocks of detonators so that they might be marked with some form of identification.

Cathal Goulding, Chief of Staff of the Provisionals, was sent for trial in Dublin on charges connected with the Explosives Substances Act and the Firearms Act. He was released on bail.

Mr. Kevin Boland's new party was refused registration in Eire.

James McDuff, arrested under the Special Powers Act, was freed on a writ of habeas corpus on the grounds that the arrest was invalid in that it did not conform to common law requirements. On release he was at once arrested under the SPA.

15 Oct. There was a two-hour gun battle between about 30 gunmen and British troops who were using explosives to crater an unapproved road.

20 Oct. Belfast students managed to keep police and Army from arresting Tomas MacGiolla, President of the official wing of Sinn Féin. He managed to escape to Eire.

26 Oct. Senator Kennedy attacked the British government for its Ulster policy, the first of many attacks.

27 Oct. Mr Basil McIver was appointed Minister of Community Relations.

28 Oct. A leading Belfast Catholic, Dr Gerard Newe, was given a Cabinet post, to try to make contact with various elements in the Catholic community.

Mr Lynch accused border patrols of deliberate violation.

1971	The British Army met armed border patrols of the
29 Oct.	Irish Army in a dispute on a border bridge. Mr Lynch protested vigorously.

The cratering of roads proved intensely unpopular.

31 Oct. The IRA blasted 8 custom-posts.

At the end of the month Mr Faulkner produced a Green Paper suggesting proportional representation, a larger Stormont Commons and a larger Senate.

Nov. Eire. The political wing of the official IRA decided at its annual conference to mount a major electoral challenge to Mr Lynch. In Ulster the police were still armed only with shot-guns and military guards had been withdrawn from police stations.

3 Nov. Irish troops were on the look-out for a coaster alleged to be carrying arms for the IRA.

The police were protesting to Mr Maudling at their lack of protection following the recent terrorist campaign against police officers and their families. Of the 12 PCs killed since 1969, 6 were killed in the last 17 days.

4 Nov. In response to near mutiny by the police, Mr Faulkner allowed the re-arming of the RUC reserves. Also military guards were returned to some stations.

5 Nov. There were reports that the Intelligence war started by the Army had begun to crack the ranks of the IRA.

The Army no longer searched areas but particular houses identified through intelligence sources.

7 Nov. Secret security moves were planned to protect Army Officers from terrorist attack, as was recently made on Major Mealyer, a retired British Army officer.

8 Nov. Mr Craig started a new group called Unionist Vanguard, meant to preserve a strict loyalist line. It contained many of the former B Specials.

10 Nov. There was great indignation when a teen-age girl was tarred and feathered in Derry for going out with a British soldier.

1971
11 Nov.
A vote of no confidence in Mr Lynch in the Dail was defeated.

12 Nov.
The first orders under the legislation were rushed through Stormont, permitting social security benefits to be stopped to pay debts to public authorities. But punishment provided yet another administrative burden.

During this week the violence included the bombing of the Woodbourne House Hotel, the cropping of the hair of three girls, the death of the 36th soldier in Ulster this year and the murder of two policemen.

16 Nov.
An IRA leader was reported to be on a major arms-buying mission. The Dutch seized a huge arms cargo at Schipol Airport.

In Eire a strong body of Communists from Eastern Europe attended the second congress of the Communist Party of Ireland.

17 Nov.
The Compton report said that there had been physical ill-treatment of a small proportion of internees.

Another inquiry, under Lord Parker, was to be set up by the cabinet to advise on possible changes in the approved methods of interrogation. Later it was announced that conditions of internees would be improved.

18 Nov.
Dublin introduced new legislation about the control of explosives, the Dangerous Substances Bill. Mr Lynch was to discuss with his cabinet the loyalty of the customs' officials following the claims of the IRA that certain officials turn a blind eye.

20 Nov.
The IRA was said to be paying a bounty of £70 for every PC killed.

Eire said it might take the case of the internees to the International Court of Justice. A Senatorial resolution co-sponsored by Senator Edward Kennedy called for the withdrawal of British troops. The State Department repudiated the statement.

21 Nov.
Mr Lynch, opening the debate in the Dail, said

1971	that re-unification was the only solution. Violence was a by-product of the division of the country.
22 Nov.	Mr Faulkner said that 85% of explosives had come from the Republic. Two women were killed in an ambush when the Army fired at a car which refused to stop at a check-point. The Army claimed that shots came from the car. The women were given IRA funerals.
25 Nov.	800 demonstrators in Dublin marched on the British Embassy after they had been addressed by Joe Cahill who threatened revenge for the two women. The rebel Parliament opened its first session. Mr Faulkner was considering talks on constitutional changes. Mr Wilson put forward a 15-point plan for Ulster. Security should be handled by Westminster; inter-party talks; ultimate Irish unity within the Commonwealth.
26 Nov.	Mr Desmond Boal called for the Unionist Party to end its links with the Orange Order. The Parliamentary Labour Party called for the end of bi-partisanship.
28 Nov.	Mr Geoffrey Johnson-Smith, a Defence Minister flew over to see the Ulster Defence Regiment. Catholic recruitment had fallen after internment. During this month, Mr Paisley formed a new party, 'Democratic Unionists' with Desmond Boal. Mr Paisley claimed that Westminster was about to introduce direct rule. This was denied by Stormont and Westminster.
Dec.	It was claimed that the IRA were holding recruiting classes and training sessions inside Eire.
2 Dec.	The IRA were offering soldiers £50 to defect. Eire spoke again of taking the case of the detainees to the European Commission of Human Rights.
5 and 6 Dec.	There were widespread police raids in Eire on the homes of the IRA including Sean MacStiofan, in connection with the death of Colonel Walker, a retired British officer.

1971 10 Dec.	Mr Paisley and Mr Boal called for the condemnation of inter-party talks with 'unification of Ireland' on the agenda. Mr Paisley had earlier denounced both internment and the ban on parades.
11 and 12 Dec.	A third member of the Ulster Defence Force was killed this week.
13 Dec.	Grenades and a rocket launcher were seized in a big haul in Ulster. An Ulster Senator was shot dead. Cardinal Conway again denounced terrorism. The Army said that almost all the original Belfast company commanders of the Provisionals were behind bars and the rounding up of replacements had begun. Mr Gerry Fitt put forward a plan for the solution of the Ulster problem involving the suspension of Stormont during which time representative groups would discuss a form of government to replace Stormont. Automatic weapons were to be made available to the RUC. The IRA hi-jacked a Canadian aircraft but were apprehended.
15 Dec.	Stormont said it would use the RUC reserve force to provide personal protection for leading Ulster citizens against attack. Joe Cahill said that the IRA were running short of guns and ammunition.
16 Dec.	Security forces found a 'fantastic' arsenal of IRA arms, ammunition and explosives at a farm near Ballymena. Mr Maudling alarmed Stormont by saying that there was little likelihood of a final military solution to the Ulster problem. An acceptable level of violence must be sought. He reassured that the constitutional position would not be changed without majority consent.
21 Dec.	The IRA bombed the heart of Belfast in an expected wave of pre-Christmas attacks.

1971 22 Dec.	A new group in the USA called the American Committee for Ulster Justice is trying to work within the American political framework to apply pressure on Britain to settle the conflict.
23 Dec.	Mr Heath made a flying visit to the troops. Cathal Goulding said that the terrorist campaign was bound to fail and that the Provisionals had begun it too early. Some UN troops were to be recalled to Eire. There was a marked increase in border checks by Irish police in the past few days. Houses in Donegal were raided by large forces of Irish police for people known to be connected with Sinn Féin. Arms and ammunition were found and three men were taken to Ballyshannon Police Station.
24 Dec.	There was a confrontation in Ballyshannon between the Irish Army, the police and a mob last night.
26 Dec.	The Parliamentary Labour Party passed a resolution which ended the bi-partisan policy on Ulster.
28 Dec.	The IRA Provisionals presented a programme: (a) The end of violence by the British Army. (b) The abolition of Stormont. (c) A free election to establish a regional Parliament. (d) The release of all political prisoners. (e) Compensation for all who had suffered British violence.
30 Dec.	The SDLP decided to pursue membership of the Socialist International, though this might strain relations with the rival Labour Party.
1972 Jan.	The Army continued to report the arrest of various IRA military personnel. The cell structure of the IRA in Belfast appeared to be broken.
4 Jan.	Mr Faulkner said that the end of internment would be decided when terrorism ended. 62 people were injured when a bomb exploded among shoppers in the centre of Belfast. The

1972	Official IRA said they would carry on their struggle for all Ireland.
	There were new moves afoot to launch all-party talks on Northern Ireland.
	The Northern Ireland Housing Executive was getting into its stride. It formally took over responsibility for future building of all publicly owned houses and flats in Belfast.
	The first Irish troops to be withdrawn from the UN force in Cyprus were preparing to leave.
5 Jan.	The BBC put on its controversial Ulster Tribunal programmes, despite the disapproval of the government.
	There was some evidence that Eire was taking a stricter line with terrorists.
	There was a third bomb attack by daylight in Belfast within a week.
8 Jan.	Troops discovered in Ulster a battalion training centre for recruits to the IRA Provisionals.
11 Jan.	Stormont was reconvened with little legislation to enact. An important provision was the appointment of a Public Prosecutor so that prosecutions would be free from suspicion of political bias.
	A further ban on marches was considered.
12 Jan.	In Eire, the unemployment figures were so high that the Opposition MPs were considering demanding an emergency debate.
13 Jan.	I.C.I. said they would include material in their gelignite that would enable the source to be traced by the Northern Ireland Security Force.
13 Jan.	There appeared to be a propaganda campaign to set the troops against each other. The Paratroops were at the receiving end of this. General Ford, G.O.C., denounced this.
18 Jan.	The ban on marches was put on for another year. The Northern Ireland Labour Party supported the ban.
	Dr Roy Johnston, a leading member of Sinn Féin,

1972   left the movement in protest at the increasing violence in Ulster.

Ulster was trying to secure the extradition of Tony 'Dutch' Docherty, IRA leader.

20 Jan.   Two Unionist MPs rebelled against Mr Faulkner's decision to ban all parades for another year. The Civil Rights' leaders who took part in the illegal marches were served with summonses. If convicted they would face a mandatory sentence of six months. The MPs who faced charges were Mr Ivan Cooper, Miss Bernadette Devlin and Mr Frank MacManus.

Since August 1969, 214 people were killed.

24 Jan.   Mr Heath met Mr Lynch in Brussels on 23 January.

Mr Faulkner said that any attempt to make a deal with the IRA would meet with total resistance.

Belfast had a sudden rise in violence, one of the 'set-piece' attacks by the Provisionals, a pattern that had occurred several times before.

25 Jan.   Royal Navy ships were operating in Northern Ireland coastal waters for four days to prevent gun-running.

26 Jan.   Mr Lynch said that the SDLP should join in the all-party talks, despite internment.

27 Jan.   Security forces in Northern Ireland believed that the IRA had suffered such heavy losses that they were turning to civil rights' marches.

30 Jan.   The banned civil rights' march in Derry took place. 13 people were killed. The Paratroopers excited odium. There was enormous indignation in the Republic, and the event attracted world interest.

30 Jan.   Gunmen killed the third policeman in two days, the 218th person to die since 1969. Catholic officers seem singled out for punishment.

31 Jan.   A senior official of the official IRA said that all members had been given freedom to shoot as many British soldiers as they possibly could in

1972	retaliation for the people killed in the Bogside on 30 January.
1 Feb.	Dublin was now prepared to support actively the alternative Opposition Parliament. Mr Lynch said that Eire might turn to other countries for aid. The IRA called for a strike in Derry. Miss Bernadette Devlin physically attacked Mr Maudling in the House.
2 Feb.	The British Embassy in Dublin was burnt. Mr Heath was considering private inter-party talks on Privy Councillor level on the problem of Ulster. A committee was set up under Lord Widgery to investigate the Derry shootings. Dr. Hillery called on the US and other countries friendly to Britain to persuade the British government to change its policy towards Ulster. He met no success. Mr Lynch, speaking of the Derry events in the Dail, referred in a conciliatory way to the Unionists and condemned the burning of the British Embassy.
4 Feb.	IRA bombers started a vengeance campaign against those who ignored the city-wide strike in Londonderry.
5 Feb.	Mr Lynch asked the IRA to keep out of the civil rights march scheduled to take place on the next Sunday.
6 Feb.	The Derry march took place peacefully, the course of the march being successfully diverted by the authorities.
7 Feb.	Mr Heath said the government would not be coerced over Ulster. The status of the province would not be changed save by consent. Mr Faulkner said that they would never surrender their destinies into the hands of the gunman or those who sought to profit from his activities. There was an increase of shootings by IRA kangaroo courts, possibly a sign of growing resent-

1972   ment among youngsters against the powers of the terrorists.

10 Feb.   The Irish courts were showing themselves alarmingly lax towards IRA defendants. Thus charges were dropped against Martin Meehan, a Provisional leader.

Dr Maurice Hayes, chairman of the Community Relations Commission resigned.

The 'Maudling' plan which included the easing of internment and enlarged Catholic participation in government was thought to be a non-starter after the shooting at Derry.

Ulster

11 Feb.   Several IRA men on the wanted list were to address a mass rally in Dublin, including Joe Cahill and Sean MacStiofan.

13 Feb.   Another march was planned for Enniskillen on Sunday.

14 Feb.   The government hoped to produce an initiative on Northern Ireland within the next two weeks.

The administration of justice was proving exceedingly difficult as a result of the huge increase in crime resulting from the political troubles.

The IRA war on troops continued. Only 3,000 people turned up for the illegal march at Enniskillen. Bernadette Devlin spoke on the inevitability of a united Ireland.

10,000 marchers, led by escapee Francis McGuigan, paraded in Dublin.

15 Feb.   The Widgery tribunal opened. Belfast had a day of bomb attacks.

16 Feb.   Mr Faulkner said that Eire would crash into disaster unless it dealt with the IRA.

A summons was served on Mr John Hume in the Bogside, by police escorted by armoured cars. Lord Widgery faced non-co-operation from Bogside residents in his enquiry.

17 Feb.   A Catholic bus-driver, a private in the UDR, was murdered.

1972 18 Feb.	200 Protestants and Catholics stayed away from work in protest at the murder of the bus-driver.
19 and 20 Feb.	The Alliance Party recruited three MPs, one, Phehin O'Neill an Ulster Unionist.

Mr. Craig held another rally at Bangor.

An internee was awarded damages for unlawful arrest against the Ministry of Defence and the Chief Constable of the RUC.

Three MPs were sentenced to six months' imprisonment for taking part in illegal marches.

21 Feb.   More reports of Eire cracking down on the IRA. Mr O'Malley, the Minister for Justice said that the men acquitted by magistrates of arms charges last week were to face trial by judge and jury for the same offences under the Courts of Justice Acts, 1936.

22 Feb.   Mr Faulkner rejected the proposals made by Mr Lynch for a new kind of power-sharing administration and an interim commission pending talks with the British government.

23 Feb.   An IRA bomb exploded at the Officers' mess of the 16th Parachute Brigade at Aldershot, killing 7 people. The event was roundly condemned. The Official IRA claimed responsibility for the dead.

24 Feb.   Cathal Goulding of the Official IRA and others were rounded up for questioning in Eire.

A Special Bill, retrospective in effect, was rushed through parliament, confirming the legality of the Army's emergency powers in Ulster. This followed the decision of a Northern Ireland Court that the Army had no authority to order the dispersal of an assembly that might lead to a breach of the peace.

26 Feb.   Mr John Taylor was seriously wounded by two IRA gunmen. The Officials claimed responsibility.

Two men were arrested in connection with the Aldershot bombing.

28 Feb.   The Dublin police freed the seven men arrested under the Offences Against the State Act.

1972	The Provisionals denounced acts of terrorism by
29 Feb.	the Officials.
1 Mar.	A sergeant of the Ulster Defence Regiment was

shot dead by two gunmen. At Westminster, Mr Reginald Maudling, pressed by some of his own political supporters to take extraordinary powers against the IRA in Great Britain, said such action was not justified at present.

2 Mar. Two more UDR men were murdered by the IRA. Special Branch in Ulster examine the possibility that some recent terrorist raids may have been the work of militant Protestants.

3 Mar. The Parker Report, signed by Lord Parker and Sir John Boyd-Carpenter, finds that 'in depth' inter-rogation methods had been used by the Army on fourteen people only and that the information thereby obtained 'was responsible for the saving of lives of innocent citizens'. The report concludes that the use of these methods could be justified in exceptional circumstances, subject to further safe-guards which it recommends. The report considers the use of these techniques in some, if not all, cases would offend against English law; but it refrains from expressing any view about the posi-tion in Northern Ireland where legal proceedings which raise this issue are pending. Lord Gardiner, the third member of the committee, considers, in his minority report, that 'in depth' interrogation methods are objectionable in all circumstances.

The government decided that techniques of in-terrogation which were found by the Compton enquiry to constitute ill-treatment (wall-standing, hooding, deprivation of sleep, etc.) will not be used in future. Questions and answers across a table will continue to be used.

Dr John Martin, principal scientific officer in the Department of Industrial and Forensic Science, Belfast, told the Widgery Tribunal that six of the thirteen who died in Londonderry's 'bloody

1972	Sunday' had probably fired weapons or handled them or had been within 30 feet of their being used.
4 and 5 Mar.	Money for IRA funds was collected at Holborn by Clann na Eireann.
6 Mar.	An explosion in a Belfast restaurant was condemned by Mr Jack Lynch and by the Sinn Féin. The provisionals blamed Union extremists.
	Mr McCausland, a Londonderry landowner and a former member of the Ulster Defence Regiment, was murdered by the official IRA.
	Mr Jack Lynch and leaders of the Social Democratic and Labour Party accorded in their view that any peace initiative must concentrate on 'concessions' to get the minority involved in a full-scale peace conference.
7 Mar.	Strong evidence emerged that the bomb blast at the Belfast restaurant on 4 March was the work of the IRA provisionals.
	At Enniskillen magistrates' court, Miss Bernadette Devlin, Mr Frank McManus and 70 other people faced charges arising from the anti-internment march on 13 February. The magistrate adjourned the case on a defence application that the court's decision could be affected by an appeal case before the High Court and rejected prosecution application that the defendants should be bound over to keep the peace until the date of the new hearing.
9 Mar.	As deaths and internment deplete the ranks of the Provisional IRA, increasing use is being made of women and of the FIANNA, the junior branch of the IRA.
10 Mar.	Eight men on arms charges were released on bail by a court at Cavan, Eire.
	The British cabinet, under pressure from military and civilian authorities in Ulster, is still discussing possible initiatives.
11 Mar.	The provisional IRA announced a 72-hour truce beginning midnight 10 March and ending Monday, 13 March.

1972
12 Mar.

An opinion poll in the Republic of Ireland showed
that a majority condemn IRA bombing and would
not insist on instant reunification of Ireland.

13 Mar.

Mr Rory O'Bradaigh, President of Provisional Sinn
Féin—hence Provisional IRA political spokesman
—said the 72-hour cease-fire was designed to
demonstrate that peace could not come about
without its political approval.

Cabinet differences between Mr Maudling and
Lord Hailsham, the Lord Chancellor, are reported
to be the cause of the government's delay in taking
any decision.

Thomas Concannon, a top-ranking IRA provisional, escaped, despite an armed guard, from a
Dublin hospital.

Mr William Craig led a rally of the newly formed
Ulster Vanguard Movement, which cuts right
across the political spectrum.

14 Mar.

The provisional IRA ended the 72-hour truce with
a wave of bomb attacks in Belfast and Londonderry.

15 Mar.

A Bogside clash resulted in three British soldiers
being wounded and two IRA men killed.

Sixteen bomb attacks have been made by provisional IRA since midnight 13/14 March. Some
arrests have been made.

16 Mar.

'Dutch' Doherty was remanded in custody in
Dublin for possessing firearms with intent to endanger life.

Mr Thomas MacGiolla, President of Sinn Féin,
and at least two other party workers, face charges
in Dublin of being members of the IRA.

Miss Bernadette Devlin and six other MPs were
among twenty-four people given suspended prison
sentences for taking part in the march at Newry on
6 February.

18 Mar.

The Army mounted a security operation in
Londonderry to capture Mr Sean MacStiofain,
Chief of Staff of provisionals, and Mr Martin
Meehan, one of the men who escaped last year

1972

from Crumlin Road jail, Belfast. The provisional IRA claimed that both men were already safely over the border.

A British Army deserter, seeking political asylum in Sweden because he objected to serving in Northern Ireland, felt others would follow his example if his case were successful.

20 Mar.

On the night of 19 March, fighting broke out between police and demonstrators who had surrounded Monaghan police station, demanding the release of three Republicans.

Massive rallies of Protestant and Catholics, objecting to any British government initiative, were addressed, respectively, by Mr William Craig, the Vanguard leader, and Mr Michael Farrell, the vice-chairman of the Northern Resistance Movement.

Pastor Jack Glass, a Glasgow militant Protestant leader, threatened that a Protestant army of 5,000 could be raised in Glasgow to fight in Northern Ireland, should the government attempt to alter the constitution of the Province.

It was reported that British students have donated more than £1,000 to the Provisional IRAs political wing since the start of internment in August 1971.

21 Mar.

There was a serious bomb explosion in Donegal Street, Belfast.

Both Mr Sean MacStiofain, Provisional IRA Chief of Staff, and Mr Cathal Goulding, Official IRA Chief of Staff, received explosives through the post. Mr MacStiofain was injured; Mr Goulding unhurt.

22 Mar.

A gun battle lasted for two hours between troops and terrorists in the Creggan estate, Londonderry. The Army estimated that twenty IRA men were involved.

23 Mar.

Mr Brian Faulkner came to London for talks with Mr Heath.

A bomb exploded in Belfast's railway station.

1972	Mr Heath announced that direct rule would be
24 Mar.	imposed on Ulster by Easter. Mr William White-

1972
24 Mar.

Mr Heath announced that direct rule would be imposed on Ulster by Easter. Mr William Whitelaw, at present Government Chief Whip, is to become Secretary of State for the Province. The main points of the political initiative are: (1) the transfer of responsibility for law and order in the province to Westminster; (2) the suspension for at least one year of the powers of the Stormont parliament and government; (3) periodic plebiscites in Ulster on whether there should be a change in the border with Eire; (4) a start on phasing out internment.

The Provisional IRA in the South claimed responsibility for the bomb explosion in Donegal Street, Belfast on 21 March.

25 Mar.

The three ministers who will assist Mr Whitelaw, Northern Irish Secretary, were named by the Prime Minister. Lord Windlesham and Mr Paul Channon are to be Ministers of State for Northern Ireland and Mr David Howell is to be Parliamentary Under-Secretary.

Mr William Craig, leader of the Ulster Vanguard Movement, called on Protestant workers to shut down the province on 27 and 28 March. If successful, he planned further 'selective' strikes at key services

The IRA leaders in Eire denied that the movement was split over Ulster strategy.

Representatives of the Social Democratic and Labour Party in Ulster were reported to have had secret talks with the Provisional IRA in Dublin. A vital proposition was reconsideration of Mr MacStiofain's call to continue the Northern campaign and a reappraisal of his snap rejection of the Heath proposals.

27 Mar.

On 27 and 28 March, a strike of almost the whole Protestant working force brought business and industrial life to a virtual halt. Huge crowds, unequivocally rejecting direct rule, attended rallies throughout the six counties.

1972
28 Mar.
Mr Seamus Twomey, the Provisional IRA's Belfast leader, has denied there was ever any question of a truce following the announcement of direct rule in Northern Ireland.

The Provisional IRA continued to vacillate over its strategic response to the Whitehall initiative.

Mr Tomas MacGiolla, President of Sinn Féin, was acquitted of charges that he was a member of the outlawed IRA organisation and that he possessed blueprints for bombs.

29 Mar.
At a huge rally at Stormont, staged to coincide with the final meeting of the Stormont Parliament before its suspension, Mr Brian Faulkner formally aligned his government with Mr William Craig and the Vanguard Movement in opposition to direct rule.

Two Roman Catholic families were burnt out of their homes after Protestant youths had set fire to a chemist's shop in Oldpark Road, Belfast.

30 Mar.
Mr Heath said his decisions had opened the way for representatives of the minority to play a constructive part in the life of the province. He said the government was 'giving attention' to the outlawing of the IRA in Britain.

1 Apr.
Mr William Whitelaw spent his first day as Secretary of State for Northern Ireland meeting senior civil servants and security chiefs. He confirmed that the ban on parades will continue for the present.

Mr William Craig has made it clear he considers the Vanguard Movement now leads the Protestant population; there are signs that his united front with Mr Faulkner is breaking down.

2 Apr.
The Provisional and Official IRA in Ulster rejected any form of direct rule, saying that they would continue to fight. Parades were held by both wings, with many of the marchers in uniform. The Army took no action.

A Roman Catholic watchman was stabbed to death

1972	in Belfast. Ten people were injured in an explosion at Magherafelt, Co. Londonderry.
3 Apr.	Thousands of Roman Catholics attending ceremonies commemorating the Easter uprising of 1916 were urged by the Provisional IRA to continue their support for the gunmen. Mr Sean Mac-Stiofain, the Provisional Chief of Staff, slipped across the border to address a rally in Londonderry, following a decision by the women of the Belfast Catholic district of Andersonstown to call for an end to the fighting.
4 Apr.	Mr Whitelaw is expected to relax the ban on parades.
6 Apr.	Mr Gerard Fitt, leader of the Social Democratic and Labour Party, appealed for the Westminster initiatives to be given a chance of success. A meeting of the Women Together Movement, which seeks peace in the province, was broken up by members of the Provisional IRA. A bomb exploded at the youth employment office in Durham Street, Belfast.
7 Apr.	Mr Justice Scarman's report into the shootings and riotings of summer, 1969, published today, says there was no plot to overthrow the Stormont government or to mount an armed insurrection. The report condemns the police in six separate incidents, but says that, in general, their courage was beyond praise. The Ulster Special Constabulary, the B Specials, showed, on several occasions, 'a lack of proper discipline in the use of firearms'. The report says that nearly everyone, from the government, the Army and the police down to individual members of each community, had misunderstood the situation in Ulster. The Provisional IRA confirmed in Dublin that it would carry on its armed struggle against Britain.
8 Apr.	Mr Whitelaw announced the immediate release of 73 internees and detainees and the closure of the prison ship *Maidstone*.

1972   Three men died in a bomb explosion and a soldier
        was shot dead in Belfast.

10 Apr. At a press conference held in the Creggan estate,
        Londonderry, the Provisional IRA said it was
        determined that Britain will never again control
        the Creggan and Bogside areas of Londonderry.
        Army commanders have long admitted that the
        areas could be retaken only at an appalling cost in
        lives. At the conference, Mr David O'Connell said
        the Provisionals would accept peace if the British
        Army were withdrawn from the streets pending
        its evacuation from Ulster; if Stormont were
        abolished; and if there were an amnesty for all
        prisoners and men on the wanted list.

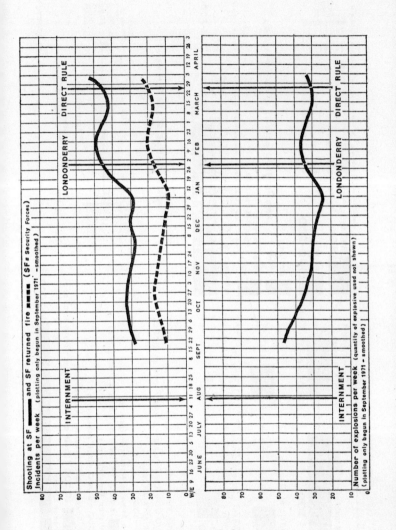

Internment and after

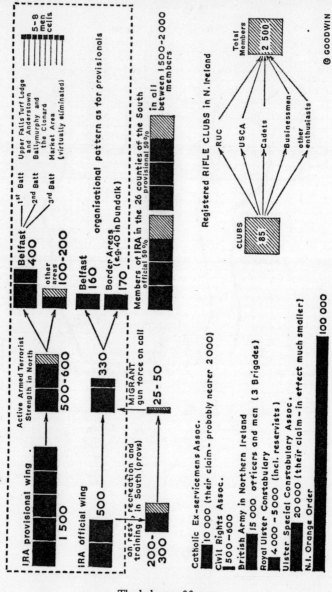

The balance of forces

1·5 M

ULSTER

Religion and Class

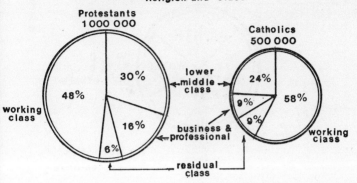

Protestants
1 000 000

Catholics
500 000

30%

48%
working class

16%

6%

24%

58%
working class

9%

9%

lower middle class

business & professional

residual class

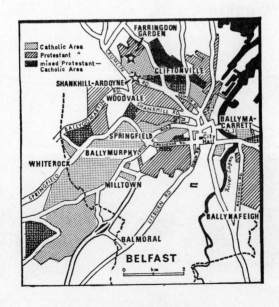

Catholic Area
Protestant "
mixed Protestant—Catholic Area

FARRINGDON GARDEN

CLIFTONVILLE

SHANKHILL-ARDOYNE

WOODVALE

SHANKHILL RD.

BALLYMA-CARRETT

BALLYGOMARTIN

SPRINGFIELD

City Hall

GROSVENOR RD.

WHITEROCK

BALLYMURPHY

SPRINGFIELD

MILTOWN

River Lagan

RAVENHILL RD.

LISBURN RD.

BALLYNAFEIGH

BALMORAL

BELFAST

0   km   2

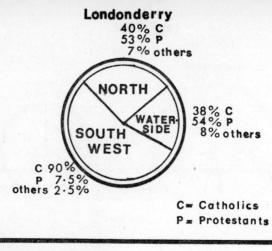

Londonderry
40% C
53% P
7% others

NORTH

WATER-SIDE

38% C
54% P
8% others

SOUTH
WEST

C 90%
P 7·5%
others 2·5%

C = Catholics
P = Protestants

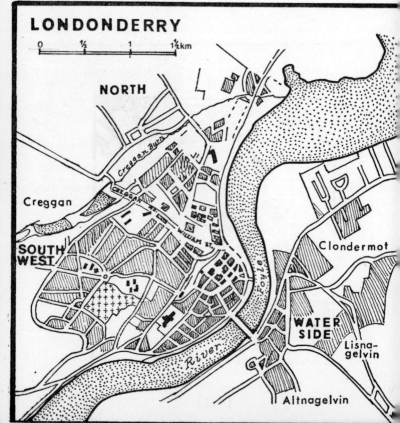

LONDONDERRY

0   ½   1   1½ km

NORTH

Creggan Burn

CREGGAN

Creggan

WILLIAM ST.

SOUTH
WEST

Clondermot

WATER
SIDE

Lisna-gelvin

River Foyle

Altnagelvin

ULSTER

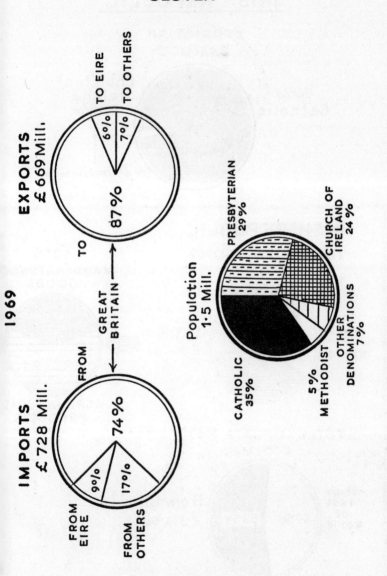

1969

EXPORTS
£669 Mill.

TO EIRE 6%
TO OTHERS 7%
TO 87%

GREAT BRITAIN

IMPORTS
£728 Mill.

FROM
FROM EIRE 9%
74%
FROM OTHERS 17%

Population 1·5 Mill.

PRESBYTERIAN 29%
CHURCH OF IRELAND 24%
OTHER DENOMINATIONS 7%
METHODIST 5%
CATHOLIC 35%

Trade and Population

[159]

IRISH REPUBLIC

Population
2 921 000

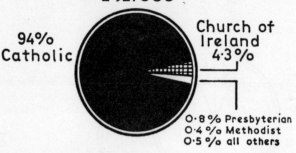

94% Catholic

Church of Ireland 4·3%

0·8% Presbyterian
0·4% Methodist
0·5% all others

IRISH REPUBLIC

TOTAL EXPORTS 1969
£ 358 Mill.

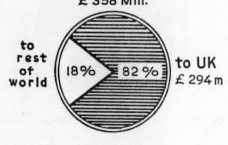

to rest of world

18%   82%   to UK £ 294 m

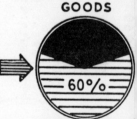

40% MANUFACTURED GOODS

60%

AGRICULTURAL PRODUCTS

TOTAL IMPORTS 1969
£ 589 Mill.

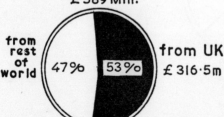

from rest of world

47%   53%   from UK £ 316·5m